GW01159261

The Reality
of
Real Estate

What a Career in Real Estate Really Looks Like
and What it Takes to Succeed

Wayne Throop

Copyright © 2024 Wayne Throop All rights reserved
The Reality of Real Estate
What a Career in Real Estate Really Looks Like and What it Takes to Succeed

Ebook ISBN: 978-1-965761-00-7
Paperback ISBN: 978-1-965761-01-4
Hardcover ISBN: 978-1-965761-02-1
Ingram ISBN: 978-1-965761-03-8

Editor: Susan Crossman
Cover Design: Alexander von Ness
          https://www.nessgraphica.com/
Interior Design: Marigold2k
Publisher: Spotlight Publishing House –
https://spotlightpublishinghouse.com

All rights reserved. You agree not to reproduce, re-transmit, distribute, disseminate, sell, publish, broadcast, or circulate any such material to any third party. We do not grant any license or rights in, or assign all or part of, its intellectual property rights in the content incorporated into this book.

Disclaimer:

There are various terms used to reference real estate professionals in this book, including "including real estate agent," "real estate salesperson" and "REALTOR®." Please note that, in Canada, only a member of the Canadian Real Estate Association may call themselves a REALTOR® and so wherever that term appears in this book please know that we are referring to a member of the Canadian Real Estate Association.

www.waynethroop.com

Endorsements

"I have read numerous real estate books throughout my career, and this one stands out. It not only helps you assess whether a career in real estate is right for you, but it also serves as a practical, tactical guide. If followed, it will pave the way to a successful career. This book is both a comprehensive real estate guide and a strategic playbook."
–Richard Robbins
CEO Richard Robbins International

"Wayne's book is a Godsend to anyone who is considering a career in real estate, who is looking to re-invigorate their career, or who is just looking to refresh their business. Real Estate is a business... and you have to treat it like a business! You need a plan... you need direction... you need a budget... you need to surround yourself with positive, like-minded people... you need to succeed! This book will help you do all of that!"
–Kent Browne
Broker/Owner/Founder of Royal LePage Team Realty

Welcome to the world of Real Estate! Wayne shares his hard-earned wisdom in a thorough, down-to-earth way helping you decide if the Real Estate game is right for you. If you are considering it, read this first! If you decide to jump in, save yourself many years and dollars by following his guidance to WIN."
–Jaime Nowak

"Wayne provides the key ingredients for what it takes to launch and develop a successful career in real estate. Weaving personal anecdotes with his knowledge and experience, Wayne offers a

comprehensive guide to not only operate in the business, but to thrive."

–Victoria Theriault
Certified DISC, GIA & TEIQue Analyst, Certified Team Facilitator

"Wayne you have written an informative and engaging guide on what it takes to be a real estate representative, anchored in real life experiences. You have included helpful details on the key aspects and competencies of the profession and have given specific guidance and pragmatic suggestions on what it takes to excel in your profession. Great job, Wayne!"

–Jennifer St. John
Language Teacher, University of Ottawa, Official Languages and Bilingualism Institute

"Wayne's book is a standout guide for anyone considering a career in real estate. Its honest, straightforward approach provides a realistic view of the profession, while it's clear, concise writing makes it a practical tool for navigating the ups and downs of the real estate world. I would highly recommend this book for anyone looking to gain a true understanding of what it takes to succeed as a real estate representative."

–Bill Martin
Sales Representative, Royal LePage Team Realty

"I love this book! It brought back so many memories of stories I had forgotten in this crazy business. This book will be a great asset for any new agent or anyone thinking of getting into the Real Estate industry. Well done, Wayne!"

–Rocco Manfredi
Sales Representative, Royal LePage Team Realty

"Through the lens of twenty years (and counting) in the real estate industry, Wayne Throop provides a glimpse inside the business and what it takes to thrive. Wayne's insights will help you to decide if this profession is a good fit for you. You might even find answers to questions you hadn't thought to ask. If you are struggling in your real estate career or just starting out, you will gain valuable knowledge of proven strategies, systems, and resources that will guide you to success, in your business and in life. As Wayne professes, the real estate environment is one of continuous learning. You will learn a lot from reading "The Reality of Real Estate". When you look back on your career in twenty years, you will be happy you did."

–Gary Weatherdon
REALTOR®, Licensed 2004

The Reality
of
Real Estate

What a Career in Real Estate Really Looks Like
and What it Takes to Succeed

Wayne Throop

SPOTLIGHT
PUBLISHING HOUSE

Goodyear, Arizona

Dedication

I dedicate this book to the women and children who benefit from the support of the Royal LePage Shelter Foundation.

THE REALITY OF REAL ESTATE
Table of Contents

Foreword

It has been a true privilege to have been associated with Wayne throughout my twenty-three years as a Broker/Owner of Royal LePage TEAM Realty.

Since earning my Real Estate license in 1983, (has it really been almost forty years?!), I have struggled with both finding my way in a very demanding business and with finding the very best training for the sales representatives under my banner. Real Estate is a tough and challenging business!!

It is tough to get started and it is challenging to keep up with the changes that seem to happen so quickly.

It is tough to stay sharp on a day-to-day basis and it is challenging to continue to improve.

It is tough to get through the highs and lows this business throws at us and it is challenging to keep a positive attitude.

It is tough to work many nights and weekends when our significant other is at home, and it is challenging to manage personal time.

I could go on!

Wayne's book is a Godsend to *anyone* who is considering real estate, who is looking to re-invigorate their career, or who is just looking to refresh their business. Real Estate *is* a business... and you have to treat it like a business! You need a plan... you need direction... you need a budget... you need to surround yourself with positive, like-minded people... you need to succeed!

This book will help you do all of that!

With true passion, Wayne has outlined many of the challenges we all face as real estate representatives... and provides great insight into how to overcome many of those same challenges. Reading this book, and putting into practice the suggestions Wayne gives you, will assist you in getting the most out of your real estate career.

I commend Wayne on sharing many personal, and sometimes difficult, events of his career... it helps us realize that while real estate is a sales-oriented business, we are all human... and prone to making mistakes, being a little lazy, losing direction, and planning poorly! To be the best, you have to learn from the best. And Wayne has proven to be the best.

Listen to him, learn from him, and become the best real estate sales professional you can be!!

Congratulations Wayne... I am confident this book will help many, many people succeed in the Real Estate business!

Kent Browne
Broker/Owner/Founder
Royal Lepage TEAM Realty
Ottawa

Introduction

Most people seem to think all real estate agents make a lot of money. Not exactly true. Would you believe the average real estate salesperson is possibly earning less than the person working in the drive-thru at your favorite fast-food restaurant? How is that even possible? If you'd like to learn more about what really goes on behind the scenes and what it is going to take to thrive and succeed long-term in the real estate business, this book is for you.

Many people who know me may be a bit surprised that I've written a book, although I've been thinking about doing this for many years and have even mentioned it to a few of my friends and colleagues recently. As I write this book, I am feeling a little bit vulnerable as I reveal a side of myself I've kept very private and shared with very few people. But despite my hesitation, the idea of writing this book just wouldn't go away. The challenge (or roadblock) was always: what exactly would I write about? How would I structure it and who would care to read it? I think what stopped me was that I just wasn't confident in how I should deliver my message.

To this point, I've always treated my personal and professional development journey as a confidential quest, and I was reluctant to share what I was doing with anyone. I didn't want to listen to those well-meaning people who might try to discourage me. You know, those negative Nellies who think personal growth is just airy-fairy, fluffy stuff for people who have too much free time on their hands. They see it as a big waste of time. They believe we should be pouring more of ourselves into our daily lives and working longer and harder at our jobs... not wasting time, working on ourselves. Now, don't get me wrong, I am not suggesting those things are not important. Of course they are. Obviously, the basic day-to-day activities we all have to take care of are important and you need to deal with them. I am a big believer in giving 100% to your career but that doesn't need to consume us. And it doesn't have to be one or the other, it can be "both... and....". In fact, I believe you can't separate the two even if you try to. My philosophy is that we need to learn more to earn more! I think entrepreneur and motivational speaker Jim Rohn said it best: "Work harder on yourself than you do on your job, and you'll go from making a living to making a fortune!"

The purpose of this book is two-fold. First, I want to help people who may be considering a career in Real Estate sales but who just aren't sure what is involved and whether they would be a good fit for this type of career. I am about to provide an honest assessment of what a career in real estate looks like behind the scenes. Secondly, I will share from my own personal experiences exactly what I believe it takes to be a successful real estate representative—and potentially make it to the top of this industry.

So why should you listen to me? What's my story? And why should you care? I've been around the real estate business since the late 1980's. I had my first introduction to investing in real estate at the age of eighteen. I was way ahead of my time back then. As far as I know, I was the only kid in high school with a mortgage. In fact, I was very much an entrepreneur from an early age. In Grade 6, I started a business selling bubble gum to kids on my school bus. It just so happened that I lived close to a corner store and many of the kids I went to school with didn't. I discovered they would pay a premium if I could pick up some gum for them and sell it to them on the ride to school.

Soon business was booming, and I began looking for ways to increase my profit margin. I discovered there was a place nearby where I could buy the bubble gum at wholesale prices which were much cheaper than what I had to pay at the corner store. I began buying the gum in bulk, at a much lower cost, and I would sell it to the other kids at retail prices (plus a small shipping and handling fee).

Soon I was earning about $50 a week, which was a lot of money for a twelve-year-old boy at the time. Unfortunately, this didn't last very long. Some of the parents began wondering why their kids were spending so much money at school all the time. Questions were being asked and one thing led to another until I was called into the principal's office. Next thing you know, my business was shut down. But that was not enough to crush my entrepreneurial spirit. In fact, it inspired and encouraged me to find other opportunities to build my fortune.

I worked hard at many different part-time jobs and small business adventures for a number of years and by Grade 12, I had managed to save up enough money for a down payment to purchase an investment property with my uncle. I provided the down payment, and my uncle did some renovations on the home, converting it from a single-family home to a duplex. You might be wondering how an eighteen-year-old high school student without a full-time job could qualify for a mortgage. Well, the short answer is, I didn't. But I was a very good salesperson, and I was able to convince my parents to cosign a mortgage loan for me. In hindsight, I am very surprised they agreed to my crazy idea, but I'm thankful they did!

My uncle and I fixed up the property (he did most of it) and we managed to rent both units in our duplex, so we were actually bringing in a monthly profit of $250 over and above our expenses, which went on for more than five years. This surplus provided me with spending money while I went to university. After I graduated five years later, we decided to sell the property, earning a nice profit of more than $20,000 each. This was a lot of money back in the early 1990s. This was precisely the amount of money I needed to pay off my student loan. So, there I was, a university graduate and debt-free at the age of twenty-three! Nice!

For about the next five years I worked for a couple of different small environmental consulting companies and eventually decided that wasn't for me. To the surprise of many people, I went back to college to get a diploma in Information Technology. After I graduated, I went for more than thirty job interviews and received five job offers, eventually choosing to join a local high-tech firm in Ottawa where I worked for the next six years.

During my time in the high-tech sector, I became very proficient at problem-solving. My boss would come to me and say *"there is a problem with this customer. I want you to go fix the problem, whatever it is. And, oh, by the way, while you are at it see if you can upsell them on some of our products and services. "*Interestingly enough, in a lot of cases, I found out we were actually the problem.

After realizing I had too much of an entrepreneurial spirit to work as an employee in a large corporation forever, I decided it was time to move on and pursue something I was more passionate about. I knew I wanted to have my own business, but I just wasn't sure exactly what that would be. I thought about this day in and day out for several weeks while I drove to and from my office. I drove the same route every day and suddenly, out of the blue one day, I spotted a sign in front of a local real estate office that said *"Thinking of a career change? Why not real estate?"*

I must have driven by that office hundreds of times before, but that one day, it suddenly clicked in my head that this was the universe's way of getting my attention. I decided to stop in and ask some questions. My excitement was back, I was on fire again! I had rediscovered my passion for the wonderful world of real estate.

Early in 2004, I made the jump and left my full-time high-tech job to start off as a licensed sales representative at a large real estate brokerage. In my first year in the business, I did a meager nine transactions, earning a whopping $35,000. No major record there! But with a strong work ethic, a lot of persistence, a willingness to try new things, and a little creativity, I was determined to figure it out.

Within two years, I was in the top 10% in my brokerage across Canada. The following two years, I was in the top 5% and then went on to the top 3% for the next three consecutive years. People would say I just got lucky. But the reality was, the harder I worked, the luckier I got. By working very hard and putting myself out there and being in the right place at the right time, good things seemed to happen!

In 2011, I was offered a management position within our brokerage, and I became a licensed real estate broker/manager, business coach, and trainer for our brokerage. I was keen to share what I had learned to help others who were struggling, and this position offered the perfect platform to do just that. But I must be honest, it wasn't just my real estate experience which enabled me to help other agents.

Everything I had done before jumping into real estate—my various part-time jobs and businesses as a teenager, my formal university and college education, and eventually my experiences working for the environmental consulting businesses and the high-tech firm—all helped me acquire some knowledge, wisdom, and understanding that I could then share with others.

A big part of my work experience has always centered around problem-solving in one form or another. I have had to learn how to work effectively with people and solve challenging problems. But the real secret ingredient in my success was not my work experience alone but my commitment to continuous learning and self-improvement along the way.

In the following pages, I am going to share what I've learned from my experiences, the books I've read, and the knowledge I've acquired through the hundreds of training conferences and programs I've participated in. I hope to provide you with some insights into what a career in real estate sales looks like behind the scenes and what it takes to make it to the top of this industry so you can enjoy a first-class thriving real estate business. My sincere hope is that you will find something of value that can help you on your personal journey and lead you toward success in whatever path you choose to follow.

The purpose of this book is to share insights into the reality of real estate behind the scenes and show what is really necessary for you to succeed at the highest level in this business as a sales professional.

This book is divided into three main sections.
Part 1 - Who are you?
Part 2 - What do you need to have?
Part 3 - What do you need to do?

My goal is that after reading this book you will be able to make an educated decision about whether or not this industry is right for you and, if it is, what it's going to take to get to the top! So, without further ado, let's dive in!

PART 1

WHO YOU ARE

Chapter 1

Is a Career in Real Estate Right for You?

More than 80% of new real estate agents don't make it past three years. Of those who quit, probably more than half of them should have never started in the first place!
—Wayne Throop

Getting into real estate is like jumping into the deep end of a pool and not knowing if you can swim. It requires commitment. If you dive in and discover you can't swim, you'll either figure it out or you'll drown. There really is no "giving real estate a try." You're either all in or you're not in at all.

The problem with real estate sales is that it looks easy! Anyone on the outside looking in can be forgiven for thinking selling real estate seems like it is a quick and easy way to make a lot of money. Maybe they have sold a property recently—or had a close friend or family member who has—and they watched their real estate agent do very little and make what they perceive to be a very large pay cheque. They say to themselves:

"That was easy!"
"If they can do it, I can do it!"
"I've got this!"
"I am going to become a real estate representative *and make a ton of quick, easy money! Fast!"*

Well, I hate to be the bearer of bad news but, unfortunately, that is not reality! If it were that easy everyone would be doing it!

Another problem with the real estate industry is that most brokerages do a very poor job of explaining exactly what is required to be successful and how much it is going to cost to get there! Many brokerages approach hiring new agents as a numbers game. Rather than hiring the right people in the first place, they'll hire pretty much anyone looking for a job knowing if they hire enough people, eventually some of them will be successful.

Perhaps Mac Anderson said it best: *"If your company's mission is to climb a tree, what would you rather do? Hire a squirrel or train a horse?"* If you ask me, the real estate industry hires far too many horses!

Many new people are lured into the real estate business by the promises of being their own boss, working flexible hours, and having unlimited income potential. Although all those things are possible for some, it is important to consider what it's going to cost to get there. Also, you should keep in mind that each of the so-called blessings of a real estate career can also be a curse at the same time. If you're not a self-motivated, disciplined person, perhaps being your own boss isn't the best idea for you. If you're not great at managing your time, working flexible hours may not mean much because you'll find yourself just working all the time. And the unlimited income potential? That may be true for a very small percentage of real estate representatives, but the reality is that most agents earn less than $50,000 per year (before expenses and income taxes). Once you take out your expenses and income tax, you'll find, as I mentioned earlier, that you are likely earning less than the person serving you in the drive-thru at your favorite fast-food restaurant. Oh, and not to mention the fact you'll very likely be sacrificing most of your evenings and weekends to do it.

As I said, the success rate for new agents in the real estate business is not great. Although the exact stats vary, some studies have suggested as many as 50% of new agents don't make it past the first year and more than 80% of new agents don't make it past three years in the business. With those kinds of numbers, it is important you think this decision through carefully before you jump in. Making a bad choice is going to cost you!

So, why do so many new agents fail in the first three years in the Real Estate business? The first, and what I think is the most obvious reason, is that many people who fail in real estate should not have started in the first place. This industry is simply not right for everyone. A common misconception is that a career in real estate sales is an easy way to make a lot of money quickly. Unfortunately, this is not true for most new agents. Success in real estate requires a lot of patience, persistence, consistency, and good old-fashioned hard work. Most people are simply not prepared or able to do what it takes to get there.

Another reason new agents fail is because they run out of money before they get their business off the ground. Remember: the average new real estate agent is earning less than $50,000 in gross commissions and, depending on your jurisdiction, it is very likely going to cost you more than $5,000 just to get your real estate license (yes, you need a license to become a real estate representative). Then you can count on expenses of at least $1,000 per month to stay in business. And that isn't going to include very much for marketing and self-promotion! (You can certainly spend a lot more). Oh, and don't forget that on top of all your business expenses you still need to keep paying the bills at home, as well (car payments, mortgage, property taxes, insurance, utility bills etc.)

How is that possible, you might ask? If you're like most people, you may have seen or heard of a real estate agent who listed a house for sale at $1,000,000 with a commission payable—as they often seem to be—of 5%. The house sold for $1,500,000 after one week on the market, having received fourteen offers. "*Boom,*" just like *that*, easy-peasy, the real estate representative just made a fast $75,000. You think this happens all the time and even if the real estate representative sells only two homes a year they're making an easy $150,000 annually.

Well, not so fast. It's time for a reality check here. First of all, do you have any idea how hard it is to get a $1,000,000 listing? This is something only a very few select agents ever do. Secondly, if an agent *is* fortunate enough to sign a million-dollar listing, it is not very likely they would be listing it for a full 5% commission (if they do, good for them). Remember commissions are always flexible. More realistically, that agent was probably charging the seller 4% ($60,000 on a sale of $1,500,000), or even less. Next, it is highly unlikely the listing agent would represent both the seller of the property and the purchaser. Meaning the buyer was probably represented by their own agent. In that case, the two brokerages would most likely split the commission 50/50. Notice I said the two "brokerages" would split the commission, not the "agents." That means $30,000 goes to each brokerage.

The brokerages would then pay the agents a portion of the commission they received. The exact split between the brokerages and the agents varies between companies, but the agents' portion usually falls somewhere between 50% to 95% of their brokerages' share of the commission, depending on the agent's experience level and commission plan.

If you are new to the business, chances are you are probably on a 50/50, 60/40 or 70/30 commission split with your brokerage. Let's be optimistic and go with 70% for this example. Now you are down to 70% of 50% of 4% of the sale price: $21,000.

Oh, but wait, there's more. Don't forget about your business expenses. For most single agents working on their own, the cost of running their business comes to about 30% of their gross income. On $21,000 that equals $6,300, which leaves you with $14,700. Oh, but you can't forget about the tax man. The government is going to want their piece of the pie, too. Depending on your income level, you're probably going to be paying something close to 40% in income tax, or $5,880. What started out sounding like an exorbitant amount of money has suddenly come down drastically and you take home $8,820.

The general perception is that the agent would have earned $75,000 on that one deal but as we've seen the reality, at $8,820, is significantly less impressive. To drive this point home even further, let's keep in mind that most newer agents do not sell even one home a year in this price range. It is far more likely they would be selling homes priced well below the $1,000,000 dollar mark, depending on the market they are in.

In fact, most newer agents sell fewer than ten homes a year so when you do the math, they really aren't earning very much, considering they have to sacrifice many of their evenings and weekends to be successful. It really is a 24/7 business and as a solo real estate agent you must be available when your clients need you.

What a real estate representative likely earns on a $1,500,000 house sale:	
House sold for:	$1,500,000
Commission of 4%:	= $60,000
Split between two brokerages:	= $30,000 ea.
Agent's portion after the split with their brokerage:	= $21,000
Agent portion after taking off 30% for business expenses:	= $14,700
Take off your 40% for income tax and you take home:	= $8,820.00

Unfortunately, many new agents jump into the business without doing their homework. They do not fully understand what it will cost to get their business to the point where they are profitable—which typically takes at least twelve to eighteen months. Without adequate financial resources, after many sleepless nights, they ultimately realize they are unable to cover their home and business expenses and, more importantly, invest in building their business. They simply "run out of runway" before their business takes off. And, the next thing you know, they quietly disappear, and you never see them again.

Another reason many people who get into real estate fail is that they aren't prepared to run their business like a business. They treat it as a job. Make no mistake about it, when you start a career as a solo real estate agent, you are very much a self-employed business owner. The minute you get your real estate license you become the CEO of your very own real estate business. As a business owner, you will need to develop systems to manage your business, and you'll need to set goals and create business plans. You'll be solely responsible for managing your time and every other aspect of your business.

Don't Take It Personally

Real estate can be a tough industry to work in. You are often dealing with people at a very emotional and stressful time in their lives and sometimes those emotions will boil over and you will bear the brunt of those emotions. You are going to have to develop some serious emotional toughness to handle these situations and not take it personally.

Two things you are going to need to succeed in real estate will be thick skin and broad shoulders. In this business there is no way to avoid it, you are going to face rejection, and it won't feel good when that happens. Someone might be rude to you or hang up the phone when you call them. One of your best friends might list their home for sale with a competitor. Your aunt Jane forgot you were in real estate and bought a home with one of your colleagues. Your favorite neighbour decides to sell their home privately. Be prepared. These things will happen, and I can guarantee you it will feel like a kick in the stomach every time it does.

When things go wrong (as they sometimes will) be prepared to be blamed for everything. When a deal goes sideways, nobody wants to take responsibility, everyone starts pointing fingers at each other and when it gets to the end of the line you might find everyone else feels like it was your fault. Whether it was or it wasn't doesn't really matter. In their eyes you dropped the ball. You can't let this get to you. You just have to let it go.

If you are the type of person who is easily offended, or you take everything personally you are going to have a very tough time surviving in the real estate business. You must become very good at letting things go and not taking everything personally. Reflect on what happened. Assess what went wrong and decide if you could have done anything differently. Learn from your mistakes and do better next time.

Finally, one of the bigger reasons many new agents fail is because they simply cannot generate new business quickly enough. This is probably the most important factor in determining how successful a new agent will be. If you can consistently generate new business, you will succeed. According to expert Real Estate Business Coach and Trainer Brian Buffini, 85% of success in real estate sales is attributed to the agent's ability to generate new leads and 15% of their success is attributed to their technical knowledge and skills. If you can be effective in finding new business, you will succeed.

A Day in The Life of a Typical Real Estate Representative:

Real estate can be a very stressful business at times (if you allow it to be). As your business starts to grow, you will very likely reach a point where you are just trying to do too many things at the same time. You may find yourself working all the time, flying from one appointment to another. It's like you're juggling chainsaws and fiery torches at the same time. You can get very busy and if you don't prioritize how you use your time, you will be spinning your wheels and running in circles. As you'll see in the story which follows, the real estate lifestyle does not always lend itself very well to making healthy choices.

Here is what a typical day for many real estate representatives might look like...

You wake up tired because you didn't sleep very well (too many things on your mind). What day is it again? Did you forget something important you were supposed to do yesterday? You slept in a little later than you should have (because you are so tired). You hit the snooze button one too many times.

You fly around the house getting ready for your first appointment. You realize you forgot to print off some important paperwork and by the time you've taken care of that there is no time for a proper, healthy breakfast. You grab a coffee and a handful of nuts and fly out the door. Traffic is heavier than usual (of course it is, you're late! Right?) Your stress level rises as you seem to hit every red light in the city. Then, the guy in the right lane flies past you just to jam in front of you before his lane ends. Your stress level goes up a little higher (*What a jerk!* you mutter to yourself. *Who does he think he is?*) You finally arrive at your first appointment five minutes late. You're stressed, but it's all good, right? After all, you are the one and only "Super-Agent!"

You fumble your way through your appointment because you didn't have enough time last night to prepare properly (you were too busy). You find out the client isn't really motivated to move any time soon anyway. It turns out they aren't even pre-approved for their financing! Too bad you were so busy you forgot to ask them about that before you scheduled your meeting with them. What a waste of time that was!

By now, you need another coffee. You pull into your favorite coffee shop drive-thru only to find about twenty cars already ahead of you and the lineup is barely moving. Too late now, you're already in line. It turns out the coffee shop is short-staffed that day and they are training a new person on serving the drive-thru customers. You try your best to be patient. By the time you get to order your extra-large double-double twenty minutes later, you are so hungry you decide you need a treat. So, you add two double chocolate donuts to your order.

Now it's time to head over to the office to do some quick research for the client who wants to submit an offer on a red-hot new listing that just came on the market. (It's their dream home and they just have to buy it). When you get to the office you get held up at the water cooler talking to other agents from your office about how busy you all are and how you never have any time. Wow! Speaking of no time, is it that late already? Where has the morning gone? You've got work to do!

You must get that research done and get the offer together and printed off for your client. Of course, the printer at the office isn't working and the Wi-Fi has just gone down. The IT guy tells you not to worry, it should be back online in about twenty minutes or so. Just about that time, your client calls you to see if you could meet them a little earlier than you had originally scheduled. (Your stress level rises again but you're trying to be patient).

Somehow you pull off a miracle and get the offer printed in time. You fight the traffic and red lights again to go meet your clients downtown to get your offer signed (they insisted on meeting in person because they weren't comfortable signing electronically). When you get there, you find out they've decided the best strategy would be to submit a really low offer so they can get a great deal... even though this is their perfect dream home, and they absolutely have to have it. "Don't worry, you've got this," they say. "After all you are the one and only Super Agent, aren't you?" You put on your smiley face and say you'll do your best.

Meanwhile, you mumble silently to yourself that you're a *hard* worker not a *miracle* worker. Your stress level rises further.

By now it's mid-afternoon and you still haven't eaten a proper meal but that's okay, you have twenty minutes until your next appointment, and you have options. There are at least three fast food restaurants within a block of where you are. You pick one and go through the drive-thru to grab a burger, a large order of fries, and a large pop. By the time you make it through the drive-thru you've only got about ten minutes left to eat; you'll have to gobble your lunch down quickly. Just as you start eating, the listing agent for the home your clients made an offer on calls to discuss some questions they have about your client's offer. Five minutes later, your twenty minutes is up, and you have to get going to the home inspection you almost forgot about. You throw the rest of the lunch you didn't have time to finish back into the paper bag and toss it onto the passenger seat. You notice what a mess your car has become, with food wrappers, paper bags, and empty coffee cups scattered all over the floor—and is that an old banana peel under the seat? And you were wondering why you had fruit flies in your car!

You pull up to the house where the home inspection is supposed to take place to find the home inspector already started examining the outside of the house before you arrived. The homeowner who insisted on being present during your inspection is fuming because you weren't there when the inspector arrived. You managed to calm them down and everything seems to be going well for the first time today. Until the inspector tells the home buyers the furnace is on its last legs and will need to be replaced before they move in.

Your buyers tell you they'll need to sleep on this news before they decide what they'd like to do. In the meantime, they'd like you to do some research for them and get them three different estimates on what it would cost to replace the furnace. Oh, and the home inspection condition in their offer must be removed before 6:00 p.m. tomorrow night.

Instead of going to the gym after work as you had planned, you now must return to the office to start calling HVAC companies to get pricing for a new furnace for your clients. Just as you sit down to start making some calls, an old long-lost client you haven't spoken with in years calls you out of the blue. They want to find out exactly what their house is worth because they are thinking about selling it in two or three years. You do your best to be polite, but they are slow talkers, and the conversation seems to drag on forever (again, you try to be patient).

By the time you get off the phone, it's after 5:00 p.m. and now all the HVAC companies are closed for the day. Oh well, you can always make those calls first thing in the morning. You're tired and hungry, anyway, so maybe it's for the best.

Boy, you could really use a snack right now. A chocolate bar or two should do the trick! Oh, and a little boost of energy would be nice. There must be some ice-cold refreshing cola around somewhere. But wait, weren't you supposed to meet that mortgage broker for a drink at the pub around 6:00 p.m.? They are sure to have plenty of clients to refer your way. You had better go. Don't forget to call your spouse and let them know you'll be home late. Boy are you ever ready for a glass of wine. What a day!

Two glasses of wine later, you decide it would be a good idea to have something to eat. That platter of chicken wings sure looks good. And those fries look like they are to die for. Your phone is blowing up with calls and text messages constantly while you are in the pub. It's hard to believe it is almost 9:00 p.m. already. You'd better get home and respond to some of these messages before you call it a day.

You get home shortly after 9:00 p.m. and your partner hands you a list of things they'd like you to do before you go to bed. They seem annoyed and remind you it is your turn to drive the kids to school in the morning and your daughter, Sally, has a dentist appointment at 11:30 a.m. You will need to drop her off at least fifteen minutes early. Oh, and don't forget the neighbors are coming over for dinner tomorrow night. Can you pick up a few groceries on your way home?

You stuff the list in your pocket and head off to respond to some of those messages you received while you were at the pub. As you head to your home office you decide you need another glass of wine to help you relax while you deal with your messages. (That makes three glasses tonight so far.) As you get started with your messages, you say to yourself: this isn't too bad. I've got this. The first couple of messages are easy and take no time at all. Then you notice a Facebook notification about one of your clients having a birthday. You had better wish them a happy birthday. One thing leads to another and the next thing you know you've just lost the last thirty minutes on social media. Is it 10:30 p.m. already? What do you have going on tomorrow? You'd better make a "to-do list" so you don't forget anything.

Let's see... "Daily To-Do List:"

1. 6:30 a.m.   Walk the dog.

2. 7:00 a.m.   Shower and breakfast.

3. 7:30 a.m.   Respond to messages from yesterday.

4. 8:15 a.m.   Drive kids to School for 8:30 a.m.

5. 9:00 a.m.   Return calls/respond to messages.

6. 10:00 a.m.   Call HVAC companies for estimates to replace furnace and follow up with buyer clients to give them information on the estimates for the furnace.

7. 11:00 a.m.   Pick Sally up at school and drive her to the Dentist.

8. 12:00 p.m.   Take Sally back to school (maybe you can grab a quick lunch together somewhere).

9. 1:00 p.m.   Meet with your broker to discuss that crazy deal at 123 Easy Street.

10. 2-4:00 p.m.   Show properties to buyer clients.

11. 4:00 p.m.   Talk to the buyers about removing the condition from their offer before 6:00 p.m.

12. 4:15 p.m.   Prepare paperwork for removing conditions in offer.

13. 4:45 p.m.   Go to the gym for a one-hour workout.

14. 6:00 p.m.   Pick up groceries for dinner tonight.

15. 7:00 p.m.   Dinner with neighbors.

16. 9:00 p.m.   Check your messages and return emails.

17. 10:00 p.m.   Shut things down and go to be early.

Wow, that sounds like a lot, how are you going to do all that in one day? You'll figure it out! After all, you are the one and only, "Super-Agent," remember? You're now running on fumes, and you are totally exhausted. A great night's sleep is exactly what you need.

Then just as you are about to head to bed, a little voice inside your head says *"wait a minute, what about the other ten messages you haven't responded to yet tonight? Are they not important? You shouldn't leave them hanging like this until tomorrow."*

Not to worry! You can get back to them first thing in the morning. It's getting late. You've had a busy day. You're exhausted and you need to listen to your body. It's time to get to bed. It's now after 11:00 p.m. Oh, and don't forget to let the dog out before you call it a night!

You brush your teeth and flop into bed totally exhausted and say good night to your partner. They seem even more annoyed now and ask you if you completed everything on the list they gave you when you came home? *"Are you kidding me right now? Did you actually forget about the list?"* You mumble that you will take care of everything first thing in the morning and say goodnight again.

Your mind is running a million miles per hour at this point, thinking about your crazy day as well as everything on your to-do list for tomorrow. You know it is time to shut down, but you are so stressed out that you can't possibly fall asleep right away. Did you forget something? When was that condition due to be removed from the offer? Finally, after you fall asleep an hour later, all you do is toss and turn all night. But tomorrow's another day. Hopefully you can get caught up!

Welcome to the wonderful world of real estate!

I've exaggerated this story (but only slightly) for effect, but truthfully some days can feel a lot like this and over time it can become very detrimental to your health.

I think anyone who has been around the real estate business for any amount of time has had many days that felt like that. I know for sure I've had plenty of days like that myself. Is it any wonder real estate representatives are not always enjoying optimal health? Think about it. Dealing with so much stress day in and day out. Being available for your clients 24/7. Not eating properly. Not exercising enough. Not getting enough sleep. It is a recipe for a health disaster, to be honest. It won't be long before your body puts the brakes on, and you get sick—or worse, come down with some type of chronic illness.

The good news is it doesn't have to be this way! You can seize control of your life, your health, your relationships, and your schedule to find a reasonable balance. You need to be prepared to manage yourself, your time, your stress level, and your diet. You need to set and maintain your boundaries. Life may not be perfect every day, but it can be manageable most of the time. Learning how to manage your time and energy effectively is one of the things you need to work on when you are focusing on your personal development. It's all about learning how to prioritize what you are doing with your time.

Chapter 2

Real Estate Is No "Part-Time" Career!

Success in the Real Estate industry
requires a full-time commitment!
—Wayne Throop

One thing I should point out is that my experience in this business over the past twenty-plus years has shown me that real estate is not a part-time career. I believe it is virtually impossible to become a great real estate agent and succeed at the highest levels doing this job part-time for any extended period. I have yet to see anyone successfully pull this off. Now, that is not to say you can't transition into it gradually from another career and work at your real estate career on a part-time basis for a few months while you are starting out, but to become successful, at some point you are going to need to bite the bullet and jump into it full time and make it your top priority.

There is an exception to this rule, however. One of the nice perks of this business, is that you can slow down gradually, as you get closer to your retirement and work part-time with just your favorite clients. Once you have gained the knowledge and expertise from a full-time successful career, then you have earned the luxury of being able to work part-time hours and still be able to earn the income you desire to supplement your retirement savings.

So, after this reality check regarding why a career in real estate sales is not right for everyone, I want to assure you it is not all doom and gloom. A career in real estate sales can be a very rewarding and lucrative career choice for those with the right attitude and a willingness to develop the necessary skills. The good news is that you don't have to be one of those casualties who drop out in the first three years. With the right guidance and direction, you can easily be among the 20% of agents who succeed and have an enjoyable long-term career in the industry. The ideas, information, tips, and techniques provided in this book, if understood and implemented, will help you get your new real estate sales career running and it will point you to the road to success in no time. If you've already been in the business for some time and you are not performing at the level you'd like to be, perhaps you'll find a tip or two here that will help you get to that next level.

Is Real Estate Right for You?

I know there are probably plenty of other assessment tools you can use to determine whether a career in real estate is right for you, but I've created the following questionnaire based on my personal experience in real estate sales and what I've learned from training and coaching hundreds of real estate professionals. Over the years, I've observed exactly what it takes to be successful in this industry so If you want to find out if you have what it takes to be successful in a real estate sales career, complete the questionnaire below.

Rate yourself honestly on a scale of 1 to 10 for each of the following statements. 1 being the least like you, 10 being the most like you.

I am generally a positive person and have an optimistic outlook on life.
| 1 | 2 | 3 | 4 | 5 | 6 | 7 | 8 | 9 | 10 |

I enjoy meeting new people.
| 1 | 2 | 3 | 4 | 5 | 6 | 7 | 8 | 9 | 10 |

I am an excellent communicator and feel comfortable talking to people.
| 1 | 2 | 3 | 4 | 5 | 6 | 7 | 8 | 9 | 10 |

I manage my time effectively most of the time.
| 1 | 2 | 3 | 4 | 5 | 6 | 7 | 8 | 9 | 10 |

I am committed to continuous improvement and seek out opportunities to learn new skills and grow as a person.
| 1 | 2 | 3 | 4 | 5 | 6 | 7 | 8 | 9 | 10 |

I am comfortable with using technology and consider myself to be reasonably tech savvy.
| 1 | 2 | 3 | 4 | 5 | 6 | 7 | 8 | 9 | 10 |

I am financially stable and manage my finances effectively most of the time.
| 1 | 2 | 3 | 4 | 5 | 6 | 7 | 8 | 9 | 10 |

I live by the Golden Rule, and I always treat others as I would like to be treated myself.

1	2	3	4	5	6	7	8	9	10

I am creative and enjoy solving problems for others.

1	2	3	4	5	6	7	8	9	10

I manage my emotions effectively and I am able to remain calm under pressure and in stressful situations.

1	2	3	4	5	6	7	8	9	10

Add up your total score and find out how likely it is you will be successful in a career in real estate sales.

If you scored lower than 60, you can stop reading any further. Respectfully, I would suggest real estate is probably not the right career choice for you. My recommendation would honestly be to save your money and search for other options that might be a better fit for you.

If your score is between 60 and 80, you still have a shot at doing this, but you are going to have some work to do. You'll need to be willing to learn and grow and work very hard but if you do, anything is possible.

If you scored above 80, congratulations, you're probably an excellent fit for the real estate business and very well positioned to succeed in this industry. If you join a great brokerage that will provide you with proper training and support, and you are willing to put in the hard work and be patient, your long-term success is almost guaranteed! Remember, building a successful career in real estate is going to be more like a marathon than a sprint.

Choose Your Brokerage Carefully

If you decide a career in real estate is right for you, probably the biggest single decision to make next is deciding which brokerage to join. Make your decision wisely. Remember, a wise man once said, *"Measure twice, cut once."* Do yourself a big favor and do your homework before joining a brokerage. What are their values? What is important to the people who work there? Do those values and priorities line up with your own?

My advice would be to come up with a list of questions that are important to you.

For example:

1. Are you a national brand or a local company?

2. How long have you been in business?

3. How large is your brokerage?

4. How many offices do you have?

5. How many agents do you have?

6. How many managers do you have?

7. Do your managers also sell real estate?

8. What type of training and support do you provide for your agents?

9. Is the training you offer created specifically for the local market?

10. Who delivers the training? What are their qualifications?

11. Is the training you offer live in class or is it virtual online training?

12. Is there any cost for the training you offer?

13. Do you offer mentoring and coaching for your agents?

14. What are the fees I would need to pay to join your brokerage?

15. Are there any other costs involved I should know about?

16. What compensation plans do you offer?

17. What sort of start-up package do you offer for new agents?

18. Is there a contract that would need to be signed?

19. Can the contract be canceled if I'm not happy?

20. Is there a penalty if I leave during the term of the contract period?

There are many other questions you could add but those are the more important ones I recommend you ask.

Once you have your list of questions prepared it is time to hit the road to go visit various brokerages. My advice would be to go unannounced. Don't tell them you are coming and see how you feel about the way people treat you when you arrive. Are they friendly when they greet you? Are they professional in the way they run the office? Is there someone available with whom you can talk?

Now, don't be surprised if the person you need to speak with is not there at the time or is in a meeting, but see how they handle the process. It is highly likely you will need to book an appointment with one of their brokers for another time but see how it goes. Remember, the way they treat you is exactly how they will treat your clients when they come into that office.

I remember when I was trying to decide which brokerage I wanted to join; it was a very difficult decision to make. All the brokerages whose representatives I spoke with sounded pretty good to me. At the time, I wasn't exactly clear on exactly what I should be looking for anyway. Every office I went to said they were the best, they had the best compensation plan, the best training and support, the best management team, and the highest market share in the local real estate market. It was hard to see through all the smoke and mirrors I was looking at. But then I stumbled upon a wise real estate representative who gave me some great advice that helped me make my decision... and he was 100% right. He said to me "There are a hundred different ways of getting paid in this business but at the end of the day you're going to be the most successful and earn the most money wherever you feel most comfortable." In other words, trust your gut.

Sometimes brokerages will make it sound like you are going to make more money joining them than if you go to some other more expensive option down the road. Be careful when considering these options. As I am sure you've experienced at some point in your life, the cheapest option isn't usually the best option. Visit each of the brokerages you are considering and see how you feel while you are there. Do their core values line up with your own? Do they treat you the way you like to be treated? Are the people you meet at that brokerage friendly and helpful? I believe you should absolutely trust your instincts on this one. If it feels right, it is probably the right choice for you.

Join a Team or Go Solo?

Once you've joined a brokerage, the next decision you're going to have to make is whether to build your business from the ground up as a solo agent working on your own or join one of the many real estate sales teams that have started over the past several years. There are pros and cons to both options so I would like to give you my perspective on some of the things you should consider before deciding which way you would like to go.

First, I should mention that I created my own real estate sales team back in 2006, when the concept of Teams was just getting started. At the time, Teams were a new thing, and most brokerages were slow to embrace the idea. Back in those days, most agents worked alone like the Lone Ranger, each doing their own thing, working pretty much around the clock 24/7.

Believe it or not, real estate can feel lonely when you work this way. I recognized very quickly that this was not the way I wanted to live my life, so I decided in my second year in the business I was going to form my own team. The first step was to get some help with the boring, tedious, admin tasks I didn't really enjoy and quite frankly wasn't always very good at. I didn't see doing all those tasks as the highest and best use of my time, so I hired my first administrative assistant and started the Wayne Throop Team.

As luck would have it, I made a wise hiring decision by hiring the daughter of a well-known custom home builder in the area. Not only was I now getting the administrative help I very much needed with my paperwork, but I was also now getting a lot of new business through the builder. Double bonus! At first, when my team was just starting, my assistant was working part-time about twenty hours a week, but this quickly grew into a full-time position. About a year later, I hired my first full-time buyer agent who focused primarily on working with our buyer clients and I began to concentrate most of my time on working with our seller clients. We worked hard as a team, and I added a new office administrator who was instrumental in helping us improve our business tracking and implement systems to serve our clients better.

Within three years, we worked our way up to being in the top 3% in our brokerage across the country. In our best year, our team sold close to $20,000,000 in real estate at a time when the average sale price wat $450,000. The reason I am sharing this story is because I want you to feel comfortable that I know what it takes to create and manage a successful team.

Overall, I would say there is no "right" or "wrong" when it comes to either joining a team or working alone as a solo agent. It really depends on you and what you are hoping to achieve in your real estate career. But here are a few issues you should consider when making your decision:

- Is there an opportunity on a team that you are interested in?
- What is your financial situation? If you are strapped for cash, it might make more sense to join a team

REAL ESTATE IS NO "PART-TIME" CAREER!

where the team leader covers most of your business expenses.

- How long could you go without income?
- Do you want to maintain your own identity in the real estate business?
- Do you have a lot of contacts?
- Are you good at generating leads?
- Do you enjoy working independently or would you prefer to work with others?
- How important is having a balanced lifestyle? If this is a priority for you then joining a team might offer you a little more flexibility.
- Do you like making your own decisions or do you prefer collaborating with others?

In many cases, the decision may come down to your financial situation and how much cash you have in a reserve fund to cover your expenses. I would say as a new agent starting out in the business, it is probably easier, and your career will take off quicker, if you join a team. I think most agents would agree. But having said that, if you are in a financial position to do so, my recommendation would be to start off on your own for the first year and get the lay of the land. Take some time to look at the various teams out there. Consider which ones you like and which ones you don't. Which teams seem to line up with your values the most? Take some training programs. Learn as much as you possibly can about the business and do your best to put a few deals together. Get some experience. Being trained and having a full year of experience in real estate will give you more to offer a team down the road if you decide that's what you want to do. And it may put you in a better position to negotiate a more favorable compensation package if you do join a team. It is also easier for a stand-alone agent who has been in the real estate business for at least a year on their own to join a team and be very successful than it would be to go the other way. If you join a team first, and then decide after a year that you are going to go on your own and leave the team, I think you are going to find it very difficult, and you might not make it.

If you find yourself in a tight financial situation when you are starting out in real estate, or if you don't have a lot of contacts to help you get started, then joining an existing team is probably the best option for you. Joining a team will provide you with many benefits. First of all, on most teams, the team leader is generally responsible for generating most of the new leads and, secondly, they will pick up the cost of the marketing expenses for the team. This means you would be focusing on serving the clients—helping people buy or possibly sell homes, and your expenses would be much lower. The trade-off is that you would split your commission with the team leader so although you would likely earn less per transaction you would probably be doing a lot more deals than you would have done on your own.

The other aspect of being part of a team I really liked was being able to brainstorm and collaborate with other team members. You have mentors on the team who will help you learn, grow, and become a much better agent. Either way, whether you decide to join a team or go it alone, there will always be pros and cons. There really is no right or wrong answer here. It all comes down to what you feel is right for you.

If you do decide to pursue a career in the real estate business, whether on your own or on a team, one of the first things you are going to notice is there are a lot of different voices out there trying to grab your attention. Each of them will offer you a range of ideas, tips, and suggestions for succeeding in this business; some ideas will conflict. It can be very confusing for a new agent trying to filter through all the noise to figure out who is right and what they should be doing. In reality, there is no one-size-fits-all approach that will work best 100% of the time for all new agents. I would suggest you consider the source of the information you receive. Is the person successful or have they been successful in the past? Do their peers respect them? What is their reputation in the industry? Does what they are suggesting resonate with you?

At the end of the day, **this is a relational business, and your success is in some way going to be tied to your ability to build and maintain relationships with people who are going to support you and your business.** If the advice you are receiving is leading you in that direction, then I would recommend you take it to heart and follow it.

After reading everything I've had to say so far, if you still think you are a good fit for this industry and you are becoming excited about jumping in, I encourage you to read on. It is time to shift gears and move on to what I believe are the keys to building a very successful real estate business.

Chapter 3

Character Qualities: The Attitude and Personality of the Ideal Real Estate Representative

If you can imagine what you would like to do in your mind and feel it in your heart, you can achieve anything you desire.
—Wayne Throop

What exactly are the characteristics of a person ideally suited to work in the real estate industry? One of the first things you are likely to notice at the beginning of your real estate career is that there really are no perfect real estate representatives. If they are out there, I sure haven't talked to them yet. One thing I can say for sure, is the majority are not anything like those polished, glamorous real estate representatives you see on HGTV or on one of the many real estate reality TV shows. Nor do they act like the pushy used car salesman everyone thinks of when you close your eyes and imagine a bad real estate representative! Most are somewhere in between.

When you are first starting in the business you will probably think most other agents around you are superstars. They are all better than you are, right? Who isn't? You're just starting, remember? You will probably think to yourself that you could never perform at their level. You can't possibly be as successful as they are. At least that is what I found myself doing. Nothing could be farther from the truth. Attitude is everything in this business. You need to have a *"can-do"* attitude. If I can do it, you can do it, too! Success is all about your attitude. You have to believe in yourself.

The surprising path to success I discovered was to focus on improving myself first.

Yes, you read that correctly! Success didn't come from becoming an expert on every form or clause used in a real estate contract. It didn't come from creating a perfect website or memorizing the Code of Ethics or the Advertising Guidelines. It came from developing myself as a person. The more value you bring to the table, the more income you will earn. It is that simple. If you want to earn more in life, then provide more value. How do you do that? You become the best version of you possible. Improving yourself is a never-ending journey. It is a process, not a destination. You can't just flick a switch and suddenly find you're the perfect real estate representative. The secret sauce leading to a high level of success in the real estate business is to work hard daily, focusing on improving yourself each and every day.

When I first got into the real estate industry back in 2004, a wise friend of mine told me, "Getting into real estate is just like joining a club. If you pay your dues, you get your membership." I didn't really get the point at the time but having been around this industry for over twenty years as a successful sales representative, a broker/manager, a trainer, and a business coach, I can now see what he meant. If you are willing to put in the hard work, success will follow!

There are a lot of fantastic real estate representatives in the business, but you will soon notice that none of them are perfect. Perfection doesn't exist in the real estate business.

Every agent has their strengths and weaknesses. Some are great at marketing and self-promotion, others are great negotiators, and many are personable and social people who are good communicators. Some are clever with how they use technology. Some are strategic thinkers, who build fantastic business plans and teams of salespeople working together towards a common goal. But none that I've ever met are great at all these things at the same time.

I like to say real estate representatives are a lot like cars. They come in all shapes and sizes. There are different styles of cars just like there are different styles of real estate representative. Some are cheaper than others. Some are more efficient. There are luxury models, sports cars, pickup trucks and SUVs. Some have features and benefits others don't have. Most will take you from Point A to Point B. But no one car (or real estate representative) is going to be perfect for every situation. Some will be more comfortable than others. Some will be faster than others. Some will be more economical than others to drive. Real estate representatives are the same. I would suggest when it comes to selling your home, you get what you pay for! You may think of real estate representatives like a bottle of red wine. You can always go with a cheaper option, but don't complain about the headache afterwards.

If I were to paint a picture of what the profile of an ideal real estate representative would look like, I would say things like they are honest, ethical, and professional. They are self-motivated and hard workers. They are laid back and easy-going, relaxed and calm under pressure. They are your rock in an emotional and stressful time. Great listeners. Social people who are caring and compassionate. They are definitely patient, persistent, and consistent. They dress sharply and professionally. They are organized, creative, and resourceful, and they are excellent problem solvers. They are life-long learners with positive attitudes. They are keen to improve their skills and increase their knowledge. They are tech savvy and willing to try new things. But most importantly of all, they have the heart of a servant, and their primary motivation is to help their clients make wise decisions regarding the largest single investment most people will ever own. They realize that the income they earn is directly related to the level of service they provide for their clients. The problem is, I've never met anyone who has had all these character qualities.

The good news is that you don't need all of these character qualities to get started. You can develop most of them over time. Don't get me wrong, the more of these character traits you may already have the better, but the most important thing you must focus on to be successful is *you*! You must be 100% committed to continuously improving yourself. Ideally you should invest one hour each day into self-improvement and personal development. In fact, a keen focus on personal development is one of the keys to long-term success in any business! But if I had to boil it all down to one single trait I believe every great real estate representative should develop, it would be a positive attitude towards life. You have to be optimistic about the future. You have to believe anything is possible! You have to believe in yourself. You need a can-do attitude. Remember, if you can conceive and believe, with a lot of persistence you will achieve. And I am here to tell you that *yes*, you *can*!

We all know nobody is perfect. But ask yourself: could you be better than you are right now? If you were to dedicate an hour a day to working on yourself, would you be a better version of yourself a year from now? I think we all know the answer to that question: yes, you would be!

The problem with attitude is that it is hard to change. If you have a bad attitude, you really can't just flick a switch and suddenly have a perfect attitude. It takes commitment to work on yourself. It all starts with awareness. The first obvious step is to recognize and accept you don't have the "right" attitude. Then you have to be willing to commit to change. It is going to take some hard work and patience. But if you work at this consistently over time, you can develop a positive attitude.

So, how do you get started if you're not already focusing on personal development? You might be thinking one hour every day sounds like a lot. You might be thinking, "I don't have that kind of time."

Well, saying you don't have time for personal development is like saying you are too hungry to eat. There is nothing else in your schedule more important than improving yourself. If you have any hope of becoming the ideal real estate representative, you have to focus on becoming the best version of you possible. You don't have to be perfect, just the best version of yourself you can possibly be. So, how do you find time for personal development? Well, I think if you were to take a look at how you use your time every day, you'd find you consistently lose or waste a lot of time.

Years ago, when I was starting out in my real estate sales career, I was trying to find more time to work on personal development and lead generation. I was always rushing around flying from one fire to the next, never feeling like I had time for anything. At the time, I was working with a business coach (yes, I hired a coach, and we will talk more about that later). My coach asked me to analyze precisely how I was using my time during a typical week. I had to record exactly what I was doing every fifteen minutes. Yes, it was a pain in the butt to do this exercise, but the results blew me away. I could not believe how much time I wasted without even noticing.

I was a big coffee drinker in those days and believe it or not I discovered I was spending nearly one hour a day in the

Tim Hortons drive-thru line up. I was also wasting close to another hour every day in what my broker/manager used to call poor "geographic time management." In other words, I would schedule appointments in various parts of the city without considering what order made the most sense considering traffic patterns at different times of the day.

By simply cutting back on my coffee intake and being a little more conscious of how I was planning my appointments, I was able to free up nearly two hours every day. I think you'd discover, if you took a careful look at how you are using your time, you'd find plenty of areas where you could free up some time you could dedicate towards improving yourself and building your business.

And now you know how to free up some time to dedicate to self-improvement, what exactly should you be doing? I recommend you start by coming up with a morning routine to start your day off in the right direction. There is a great book on this topic, written by Hal Elrod, called *The Miracle Morning*. This would be an excellent place to start if you want some ideas on what you might include in your morning routine. But other than that, I suggest you focus the first hour every day on getting your mindset in the right place through meditation, reflection time, journaling, expressing gratitude, writing out affirmations, prayer, reading a good self-help or motivational book, listening to a motivational podcast, and exercise.

Keep it positive and take in only the good stuff. No negativity. Avoid going doom scrolling on your social media platforms and watching or listening to the news. It is hard to start your day off being positive if you are focused on all the misery the media constantly blasts out. Why worry about things you have no control over? If you want to improve your attitude, be conscious of your mental diet. What are you taking in on a daily basis?

Journaling:

Personally, I have found journaling, a key part of my personal development journey, to be a powerful tool to help unload all the baggage from my mind. There is usually a lot of mental clutter taking up space in our heads. So, whenever I am dealing with challenges, I just write about them. I've been doing this for at least twenty-five years. I remember when I was a young boy, I once found a notebook my dad had written some notes in when he had been a teenager, and I thought that was very cool. It was like a message from the past. I would say that is what inspired me to start writing in journals. The nice thing about journaling is you can write whatever you want. Sometimes it might make sense, other times maybe not. Sometimes you're complaining, other times you're expressing gratitude. Sometimes, you might write a story, other times a conversation with yourself. You can literally solve all the world's problems in your very own journal.

Over the years, I've written thousands of pages of notes. The funny thing is, I rarely go back to read what I've written. For me, the primary benefit of journaling is the process of writing, not what I actually write about. I find it therapeutic.

I remember a time when I wrote in a journal for six hours straight on a flight from London, UK, to Montreal. The time just seemed to fly by in the blink of an eye. When my father passed away in 2018, I wrote more than fifty-eight pages in my journal in one weekend. I wrote about all the good memories I had. The things I wished I had said that I didn't. The things I wished I had done that I didn't. I wrote about what I liked about my dad and what I didn't like. The good times and the bad. I covered everything I could possibly think of related to my memories of my dad. Interestingly, I really didn't have many regrets. But somehow, this exercise of writing everything out in my journal was very therapeutic for me. And the funny thing is, I've never once gone back to my journal to read all those notes I wrote that weekend. Who knows, maybe one day I will, but for me the real value of writing in my journal is just to download all my thoughts, concerns, troubles and let them go.

There are no real rules when it comes to journaling. All you have to do is write down whatever you are thinking about. Whatever thoughts come to mind, just write them down. You should try this the next time you are feeling overwhelmed or stressed. You don't have to worry about proper grammar or writing complete sentences. Sometimes I find my mind goes faster than I can write so my pen is three or four thoughts behind my thinking. I often write bits and pieces of different thoughts, but I don't let that bother me. I just keep going as fast as I can.

You might want to start your day off by writing about all the things you are grateful for. Maybe write out some affirmations. There are plenty of benefits in taking the time to write regularly in your journal. I would highly recommend it, and I think you'll find it to be an enjoyable and worthwhile pursuit that will become a cornerstone of your personal development journey. I suggest you give it a try. Afterall, what do you have to lose?

Reading

"Learn more to earn more!" If you're not already an avid reader, it is time to get started becoming one. You can easily become a regular reader by starting to read for just fifteen minutes every day. Each week you can add an extra five minutes until you're up to one hour. I typically have an on-going goal to read at least one book that is going to help me improve in some way every month.

The first book on my personal development journey was an easy read called *"The Maverick Mindset"* by Doug Hall. It ignited a keen interest in personal growth and development inside of me that continues to burn to this day. I have now read more than 100 books, typically focusing on personal growth, spirituality, business, and health and wellness. Each one has contributed in some small way to helping me to become a better version of myself.

I have read many of these books multiple times. My favorites tend to be very used up by the time I finish with them. When I get into a book, I devour the content. I highlight key points. I write notes in the margins. I dog ear my favorite pages. I even make notes in my journals about the content. I find it is easy to read the content and understand the concepts, but it is an entirely different matter to put those ideas into practice in daily life.

The present moment is where the rubber hits the road. I must be a slow learner because I've read some of these books five or six times and I still haven't been able to put everything into practice in my daily life. Yet I persist! I just keep going at it and this is one of the reasons why I've been successful. I persist until I succeed. I try repeatedly, until I develop new habits and slowly change who I am. Bit by bit, one tiny change at a time. The people around me on a daily basis barely notice most of these changes but over the years they've added up to massive change and improvement!

When I consider what my income was when I started this journey of personal growth and development to where I am today, I am now earning at least four times what I used to earn. Like I said, the income you earn is directly related to the value you bring to the marketplace. Learn more to earn more!

Spirituality

There is no way around it, part of your personal growth journey is going to include your spirituality. There is nothing here to be afraid of. Just get curious and ask yourself what you actually believe. What is your role in the grand scheme of life? Why are you here? How are you connected to others? What small part can you play in making the world a better place?

What exactly is spirituality? I suppose there are a lot of different points of view on this topic. Many people give very little attention to spirituality. Some might even argue it is a bunch of hocus-pocus, and not worthy of our time and attention. Many others confuse spirituality with religion. I can assure you the two are very different.

A religion is a group or community of people who share a specific set of organized beliefs and practices. Religion gives its community of followers a set of rules and principles to guide their behavior. Spirituality is more of an individual practice and has to do with finding a sense of peace and purpose for your life. Spirituality is about finding your connection with the divine power of the universe (however you may define that). You don't have to be religious to be a spiritual person. My suggestion would be to find a quiet space where you can relax and reflect on what exactly you believe about the universe and why we are here. Get curious about it. I believe your spirit is part of who you are and if you want to grow as a person, you can't avoid exploring your spiritual side. It is just part of who you are.

Health

I've heard it said many times over the years that your health is your greatest wealth. Without it nothing else really matters.

Think about it. What good is all the wealth in the world if you have given up your health to get there? You have to look after the goose that lays the golden eggs. And if you didn't already know this, you are the golden goose for your business. If there is no goose, there are no golden eggs!

I spent the first half of my life abusing my body and not taking care of my health and now in the second half I am spending a great deal of my time, effort, and money trying to fix the mess I created over the years. If only I had learned sooner! My health was great until my early forties, or so I thought. Little did I know, there were a number of health issues lurking just below the surface waiting to catch up with me. As we get older and hopefully a little wiser, we realize that those things we thought we were getting away with as teenagers and twenty-somethings are now showing up as health problems later in life.

All those late nights drinking too many beers. The all-nighters before a big exam when we were in school. Those crazy ski trips and nasty falls on the ski slopes. The wipeouts on a mountain bike. They may not seem like much at the time when you're young, but they do come back to haunt us as we get older.

A big part of your personal development journey is going to involve learning to pay attention to your body. How do you feel? What is working and what isn't working? Learn what you need to do to maintain a healthy state of mind and body. What do you need to eat on a regular basis? What should you be avoiding?

The first step in this process of change is always awareness. Ask yourself how you are doing. Do you have energy? Do you sleep well at night? Are you sick very often? If you are not where you want to be, do something about it. If you are looking for a good place to start, I would recommend a book called *The Rain*

Barrel Effect by Dr. Stephen Cabral. Educate yourself on good nutrition and lifestyle choices. Learn what you can do to get yourself back on track if you have drifted off course with your health. It's important to look after yourself. Do yourself a favor and make your health a priority before it's too late.

Chapter 4

Financial And Personal Relationship Boundaries

Your finances and your personal relationships go hand in hand, and you should manage both very carefully!
—Wayne Throop

Although I am not a professional accountant, I believe there is one area you absolutely must become keenly aware of at all times and that is your financial situation. Both in your business and in your personal life. If you already have a good handle on your finances and your budget, that is great. Good for you! But my experiences working with real estate representatives over the years have shown me that is more the exception than it is the rule. Most real estate representatives don't seem to do a very good job of tracking their expenses and separating their business expenses from their personal expenses. The two areas get blurred together. They also don't seem to have a budget or know how much of a profit they are earning from their business.

This is something you will need to master if you want to truly to become a successful real estate representatives, Get good at budgeting and tracking your expenses and knowing where you stand financially at all times. If this is not your thing, then go get some help. Hire a professional accountant.

I know there are plenty of great courses and training sessions available to improve your knowledge and skills in this area, but I do have a few tips to help you get started:

1. Create a personal budget and a business budget.

2. Deposit your paychecks into a business account.

3. Pay yourself a salary from your business account and directly deposit it into your personal account.

4. Set aside money for taxes from every paycheck.

5. If you are in Canada, set aside your HST money in a separate account. In other jurisdictions, you may have a similar business tax that must be allocated to your government.

6. Hire a professional accountant to prepare your tax returns.

7. Track all your expenses consistently (both personal and business).

8. Prepare quarterly Profit and Loss statements.

9. Always have a set of written financial goals.

10. Create a business plan annually and review it quarterly.

One thing you must be prepared for is the financial ups and downs that happen all the time in real estate. One month you might close five or six transactions, and you just made $80,000 or $90,000 in gross commissions and then all of sudden the gravy train sputters, and you don't close another deal for the next three months. You have to be good at managing your expenses, so you are setting aside enough money when you get those big pay checks to cover you during those months when you don't have any income. You also need to be able to manage the emotional highs and lows caused by that inconsistent income stream. From what I've seen, there are a lot of real estate representatives who aren't very good at this.

Here is an example of what this might look like for a typical real estate representative. After a few months of consistent effort and hard work, they put together a couple of deals. They are pretty happy with themselves and start to build up a little momentum. Suddenly, they get a little busier and they do a few more deals. Suddenly, they are riding high. They have a lot of confidence. Things are really going their way. Maybe they've just put together ten or twelve deals in less than two months. *"This business is great!"* they say!

Unfortunately, there is often one small problem that starts to creep up during this time at the top. When they get busy doing deals, they stop doing the things they were doing to generate new leads and fill their pipeline with future opportunities. Nevertheless, they carry on. They forge ahead, focusing on the next deal. They are not worried about generating new leads right now. They have way too much going on. Besides, they need to celebrate their success. They decide to treat themselves to the beautiful new sports car they've had their eye on. Sure, it's a lot of money but they've just brought in more than $100,000 in gross commissions in the past few months and there's plenty more where that came from. (Or so they think.) Next year is going to be even better than this year was.

About this time, their pipeline of new leads is starting to look a little sparse. A few opportunities slip through the cracks. A couple of people change their plans and decide not to move. And the agent has not been doing very much to generate any new leads because they've been too "busy" to invest any time in trying to find new business. Suddenly, the market starts to cool. Interest rates are climbing. Inflation has become a problem. Oh, did I mention tax time is just around the corner? Guess what? It is entirely possible the agent could owe more than 50% of the $100,000 they just earned to the government for income taxes.

Now that they've already spent the money on that new car, they don't have enough left to cover their tax bill, not to mention their regular ongoing business expenses or their personal living expenses. Maybe that new car wasn't the best idea? Now what? They have no leads, there are no deals happening, and they owe more money to the government than they have in their bank account. The agent's stress levels are going through the roof, and they have to go back to square one and start the whole process over again. They must get back to focusing on doing those daily activities they were doing consistently that helped them get so busy. And the bad news is that it is going to take some time. You don't just flick a switch and suddenly new leads start pouring in. You must be consistent for an extended period before you see the results.

The moral of this story is that you need to have a daily focus on generating new business and managing your finances responsibly so you can carry yourself and your business through those quiet spells that will inevitably happen over time. If you plan to be successful in real estate, becoming effective at managing your finances both personally and professionally is going to be critical. There is no point in working hard to earn a lot of money, only to see it evaporate and finding you have no idea where it all went. Educate yourself on how to manage your money. You don't have to be an expert but at least learn the basics and then hire professionals to fill in the gaps. Hire a bookkeeper to take care of organizing your business receipts and tracking your expenses. Get advice from a financial advisor about saving and investing your money wisely. Talk to an accountant about tax planning. Talk to a professional to find out if forming a Personal Real Estate Corporation (PREC) makes sense or is an option for you. If you plan to make it to the top of the real estate industry, these professionals need to be part of your team.

Personal Relationships

A career in real estate can often lead to a real train wreck for your personal relationships if you're not careful. Trust me, I can speak on this subject from my own personal experience. The best possible advice I can give you is to be very careful to make sure you are conscious of your personal relationships and where you are at with them every day. I want to share a cautionary tale I hope might help someone else learn from my mistakes.

When I first got started in real estate, I was told to be careful because this business is notorious for causing relationships to end in divorce. At the time, I thought that would never happen to me. I was happily married. I managed to maintain a healthy balance between my real estate career and my relationship with my wife. No problem. Well, it turns out there *was* a problem and the worst of it was I didn't see it coming until it was too late.

By the time I started my real estate career, I had already been married for about seven years. I had a great wife who was a professional engineer with a solid job and a great salary.

We always got along great. We never argued about anything. We were both very independent people but enjoyed spending time doing things together. For the most part, my wife was a very easygoing person. Unfortunately, that turned out to be part of the problem. She was too easygoing. As my career in real estate started to take off, I was focusing more and more attention on my business and less and less on my relationship with my wife. At the time, she was doing the same in her career and we had no children. Both of us had tunnel vision focused more on our careers and less on each other.

As I became busier, I found myself either being late for everything I had planned with my wife or, even worse, having to cancel plans at the last minute due to work commitments. For the longest time, she always said,

"No problem."

"Don't worry about it."

"No big deal."

"We can go another time."

I became complacent. I began to take our relationship for granted. I became obsessed with my own career and the success of my business, and I lost sight of my personal relationships. I was not conscious of what was going on in my personal life until suddenly one day it all came to an abrupt end. We sat down just after Christmas and had a discussion about where we were at, and she said she was done (and she was).

"No problem" suddenly became a huge problem, and my marriage was over. I very quickly realized the opportunity for me to fix things had long since passed. I had been asleep at the wheel and missed all the warning signs leading up to that day. I was too absorbed in my career success and achieving that next sales award, and I had given very little attention to my marriage. I don't want this to happen to you.

Here is a story I remember very clearly that was probably one of the final tests of my soon-to-be-ex-wife's patience. This was the first time I could recall her showing any type of frustration with my career and how I was managing my real estate business. (I should have paid more attention). At the time, I was working with a rather difficult elderly client I will call, "Norma." Norma was not your average pain-in-the-butt client. She was extreme in every way. She was an elderly widow downsizing and moving from a single detached home into a condo. Things all started to go south when I listed her home for sale. It was a modest bungalow in good condition but her asking price was a little too optimistic for the market at that time (in other words, it was overpriced). In any case, she lived in an area where I liked to do business, so I was excited about having her listing, overpriced or not.

While I had her place listed for sale, she asked if I could show her some condos in two very specific buildings. She had made up her mind that was where she wanted to live and wasn't interested in seeing any other places. Not only had she decided which building she wanted to live in, she had also decided which side of the building and which floors she would consider.

Unfortunately, Norma did not drive so she would call me every time a new listing came up in one of the two buildings she was interested in and ask me to take her to see them. This entailed about an hour of driving time for me each time. Norma wanted to see every single unit that came up for sale in either of those buildings, even if they didn't fit her criteria. She insisted on going to see many of these units multiple times, even though they were not a match for her. She also had plenty of questions about every single unit I showed her, which required me to spend a significant amount of time researching. Another interesting part of this story is that Norma was not in a position to buy a condo until her other home was sold, which wasn't happening very quickly because our asking price was too high.

Unfortunately, at this point in my career, I hadn't learned to set boundaries yet, and I was just running myself ragged managing this one difficult client. But there came a day when I thought I had figured it all out. It was my anniversary. My wife and I had planned a nice romantic dinner with no distractions that evening. I even had another real estate representative lined up to cover for me. Knowing Norma was very needy and high maintenance, I called her early that day to let her know it was my anniversary and I was planning a special dinner with my wife that night so I would be taking the evening off. I specifically told her I had another real estate representative covering for me and I asked her if she had any questions or if there was anything else I could do for her before I finished for the day. "No, I'm fine. There is nothing I need right now," she said. "Enjoy your evening." (Famous last words).

Feeling relieved that she was taken care of, I thought I was good to go, and the rest of the night would fall into place perfectly. But no, it was just not meant to be. Around 6:30 that evening my wife and I were just starting to enjoy our first glass of wine to celebrate our anniversary when suddenly my phone started buzzing (I had turned off the ringer, but it was on vibrate mode). At first, I ignored it, but it kept going. It would stop for a few minutes then start again. Over and over. It just kept going. In the span of less than an hour, Norma had called four times, paged me twice and sent me an email.

Just Answer the Damned Call!

At first, my wife seemed fine with what was happening, but I began to notice a look on her face that told me she wasn't fine. After an hour of listening to my phone buzzing every few minutes, with me trying to pretend I wasn't distracted, she finally blurted out, "Just answer the damned call! Obviously, there is some kind of real estate emergency you are going to need to deal with." Once I realized it was Norma, I knew she wouldn't quit until she talked to me. Finally, I agreed with my wife and excused myself to speak to Norma.

My wife was very frustrated I couldn't give her my undivided attention for even a single evening. This was the first time I could recall her being visibly upset about my real estate business. She wasn't one to complain very often but she didn't have to say a word that night, I knew by the look on her face she was very disappointed. I feel like I don't even really need to tell the rest of the story, but I will, just to confirm what you are probably already thinking.

What was so urgent that required Norma to interrupt my special anniversary evening? Well, I would hardly call it urgent at all. She was calling me because a new condo listing had just come up that day and she wanted me to book a showing appointment for later that week. I tried my very best to be patient and professional when I called her back, but this was a tough one for me to swallow. In hindsight, it was probably the beginning of the end of my marriage. Unfortunately, at that point in my career, I just couldn't maintain my boundaries and take control of my business, nor was I aware of what was starting to happen in my relationship with my wife. I was so absorbed in my real estate business that I was completely neglecting my personal relationships.

Thankfully, most of the clients you will work with will not be like Norma. You simply can't afford to work with very many like her. Not if you value the personal relationships you enjoy with your family and close friends. Also, for the sake of your own mental health, trust me, it's just not worth it. If you start to get the feeling that someone is just not a good fit for you, trust your gut. It's time to say goodbye!

There is one observation I'd like to share that I had to learn the hard way. The people who are the most difficult to work with, who won't listen to any of your advice, who are the biggest pains in the butt, and who don't appreciate anything you do for them are also the exact same people who insist on a discount off your commission. How about "No!" Don't force yourself to work with those people.

As hard as it is to understand when you are first starting out in real estate, you need to say no to some clients and always make your personal relationships and your own mental health your top priorities. Don't ever sacrifice yourself and what is important to you, just to pacify a client. Awareness of the state of your relationships is the key. My best advice is to always pay attention and be conscious of what is going on in your relationships. Don't allow this or any other career to take priority. Life is too short. When you are dead and gone no one is going to care how many houses you sold, what sales awards you won, or how much money you made. They are going to be talking about the relationships they had with you and how you made them feel. My advice for you is to always make your personal relationships your top priority.

As part of your personal development journey, you should always work towards becoming a more conscious person, a better partner for your spouse and the best possible version of yourself. You'll hear me say this often, but awareness is always the first step towards change. You need to be aware of problems that may be developing so you can address them while they are minor issues and long before they become serious deal breakers. If you want to live a more conscious life, my suggestion would be to incorporate a meditation practice into your daily routine. Work hard to live your life consciously.

Always pay attention and show your appreciation for the love and support you get from your family and those who are closest to you. Never take those relationships for granted. If you do, you might find one day they are gone and they are not coming back. Learn from my experience. Please don't make the same mistakes I did.

Chapter 5

The Identity Shift Involved in Becoming a Great Real Estate Representative

It's going to take patience, persistence,
professionalism, and a lot of good old-fashioned hard
work to succeed in the real estate business!
—Wayne Throop

I feel there is a need to elevate the level of professionalism in the real estate industry. You have to be serious about your career, working hard to provide exceptional service and being a true professional, not only when serving your clients, but also in your interactions with other real estate representatives, and especially your office administrators. If you want to be a professional, there is an easy formula to follow. Treat others the way you'd like to be treated yourself. It really is that simple.

As a starting point, I invite you to do an honest assessment of yourself and get curious about what your true motivation is for being a real estate representative. Why did you get into the real estate business in the first place or, if you're not already in the business, what is it about real estate that appeals to you? Be honest with yourself. Is it simply to earn a lot of money? Is it because you like to look at houses? Maybe it's because you like the flexibility this type of career offers. Maybe you want to invest in properties. Maybe you had no other good options, so you thought you'd give real estate a try. Or do you have a sincere desire to help others, and you want to help people make wise decisions when making the largest single investment decision they are likely to ever make?

If you want to understand what you might need to change about your approach to your life it is important to know your starting point. This is going to require some introspection and self-reflection time. I know this may seem a little unusual at first if it's not your thing. It's something most people don't do on a very regular basis. It may not be easy, but do yourself a favor, grab your journal, find a quiet space where you can be alone, get rid of your cell phone and any other distractions for an hour or so, and dial in to your thoughts. Ask yourself the question: "Why did I decide to become a real estate representative?" Begin writing down whatever comes to mind. You might be surprised by what comes up. It is important to be honest with yourself. There is no point writing down what you think are the "right" reasons. Just listen to yourself and make notes. There are no right or wrong answers. You are who you are, and your motivation is what it is. Once you are more aware of the true reasons you are in this business then you have a starting point. You can build from there.

The end goal here is to get to a place where you focus 100% of your attention on serving your clients to the highest possible level regardless of how much work is required and how much you are going to earn as a result. You need to get to a place where your entire focus is on how you can improve the services you provide for your clients. Ask yourself, *What more can I do? How can I get better What else could I do? What are my clients looking for?* It's important to realize there is no perfect end destination you are going to reach where you can stop trying to improve and expand the services you provide. You must be able to adapt to your clients' changing needs. Get creative and think outside the box. If you are not sure what to do ask your clients what they would like.

The real estate business is constantly evolving and it's changing rapidly, perhaps more than almost any other industry outside of high tech. New challenges arise, almost daily. The rules change. New regulations are implemented. New technologies are introduced. New business models suddenly appear while others disappear. New industry disruptors arrive on the scene. You are going to have to pivot and adapt to those changes. Throughout your career, you may need to reinvent yourself several times, change the services you provide, and even change the way you deliver those services. This is just the nature of real estate. It is a never-ending process, one that requires a mindset shift. If you're not already, you will need to become adaptable, flexible, and willing to change. If not, you will fail.

I can share a story from my experience in real estate sales that will illustrate just how much the real estate business has changed in the past few years. In 2005, I was selling a home that was about a forty-five-minute drive from my office at the best of times. It was pretty much on the exact opposite side of the city, diagonally across from where my office was located. There was no direct route from my office to this home. When I had to drive to the house, I had two choices. I could either drive down a major highway cutting through the core of the city. (Which at certain times of the day during peak traffic times would be an absolute nightmare and take well over an hour). Or I could zig zag my way around the outskirts of town, through a series of country roads and take my chances around getting caught behind slow-moving farm machinery, dump trucks, snowplows or school buses. Either way, it wasn't an easy, nor a quick drive.

To make this story even more interesting, I had this listing during the winter months and as fate would have it, the night

I received my first offer on this property, there was a bad freezing rainstorm. Unfortunately, I was dealing with a less-than-reasonable agent on the other end who was representing the buyers. They insisted on dealing with this offer that night. Apparently, the buyers were from out-of-town, and they were only around for a few days; they needed to make a quick decision so they could secure a home before they left. If this one wasn't going to work out, they were prepared to move on quickly.

Now, in those days, signing paperwork electronically was not really a viable option. In rare situations, if your clients had the right technology in their home, you could print the offer, scan it to make it a PDF document, attach it to an email and send it to your clients. Once they receive your email, you would ask them to print the PDF document attached to the email. Once they had a printed copy, you would explain where they should sign the documents. Once they understood all the terms and conditions, they would sign everything, then scan the signed document back into a PDF document and email it back to you as an attachment. All of this required several miracles to pull off successfully. First, the client had to be reasonably tech savvy. Next, they had to have a home computer, a printer, a scanner, and, of course, a reasonably decent connection to the internet. Back in 2005, technology was not what it is today, and most people did not even come close to meeting these requirements. Certainly not my clients in this situation. So, what did I have to do? I printed off all the paperwork, jumped in my car, and drove all the way across the city in the middle of a freezing rainstorm to meet my clients and get the documents signed. I drove for more than three miserable hours that night to get those signatures and get that deal put together.

Did I really want to get in my car and drive more than three hours in a freezing rainstorm? Absolutely not! But I knew it was in my clients' best interest to sell their home as soon as possible, so I did what I had to do at the time to get the job done. That is what true customer service really looks like. You simply do whatever it takes to serve your clients' best interests. And if that means driving more than three hours in a freezing rainstorm, so be it. That is what you have to do.

How would that exact situation play out today with all the advances in technology and the advent of electronic signatures? It seems to me that people are far more tech savvy today than ever before, so most people are reasonably comfortable using technology. Today, almost everyone has a computer or some type of electronic device in their homes and a decent Wi-Fi connection to the internet. Right from the start, the whole process is going to be much easier than it used to be. You would simply prepare the required documents and send them electronically to your clients using a digital signature platform. They would open the documents, and you would explain everything to them by phone or via Zoom or other similar video conferencing technology, to make sure they understand everything they are signing. Within a few short minutes, they have signed the documents and sent them back to you. Easy-peasy. Just like that, you're done, and you didn't even need to leave your home office. Instead of driving three hours in a nasty freezing rainstorm, you could sit inside your cozy home office, sipping your green tea, looking out the window enjoying how beautiful the ice building up on the tree branches looks. What was once a three-hour-plus, potentially dangerous ordeal back in 2005, has now turned into a much easier (safer) and much less stressful situation that can easily be completed in just a few minutes.

Like I said, the business is constantly changing and evolving. Imagine just how much of an impact something as simple as clients being allowed to sign legal documents electronically has changed the real estate business?

One thing I can predict with absolute certainty is that this business will continue to change rapidly. If you plan to have long term success in the real estate business, you will need to be okay with that. This one is a dealbreaker, folks. You simply must be flexible and willing to adapt and change as the business changes. If you're the type of person who resists change and is reluctant to learn and adapt to new technology, I've got to be honest, you are going to struggle in this business and you simply won't be able to stay at the top level for the long term.

Perhaps you already believe you have the heart of a servant, and your sole purpose is to help people. That's a great starting point, but my guess is there is still room for improvement. Get curious. Ask yourself, "what else could I do?" If you really want to get real, ask your clients what else you could be doing to help them? What other services could you provide for them? How could you streamline the process and make it easier for your clients? What new technology platforms could you be learning and implementing in your business to speed up the home buying or selling process? If you can train yourself to think this way and make it a habit to stay focused on constantly improving yourself and your services, I can guarantee you, the income will follow automatically. Remember—the income you earn is directly related to the level of service you provide. Providing better service will always translate into earning more money.

What Can You Change and Which Issues Are Deal Breakers?

The good news is that you don't need to be perfect. You don't need every single one of the character traits and skills an ideal real estate representative has just to get started in this business. Some of these traits and skills are more critical than others. But you do need to be willing to work hard on the areas that don't come naturally for you. Maybe you're not naturally good at negotiating. That's fine, you can learn how to do that. Maybe you're not a great public speaker and you're scared half to death to get up and speak in front of a group of people. You can join a public speaking organization like Toastmasters to get more comfortable with the idea.

Maybe you don't know a lot about marketing or selling. No problem, you can fix that with some training and mentoring from your brokerage. Maybe you're not always the most punctual person. You can work on that. Maybe you're not a naturally patient person. That is a skill or ability you can develop over time. Maybe you're not great at managing your time effectively or being organized. Again, not a problem. Those are skills you can learn to become good at. Maybe you don't know the first thing about creating a budget and managing your finances effectively. No problem, that can be fixed through some education and training.

These areas all have one thing in common: they are all necessary to succeed at the highest level in the real estate business. The good news is that if you are not already strong in these areas, you can roll up your sleeves and go to work on yourself. Make no mistake, your success is going to require your focused attention and a strong conscious commitment to get better in those areas... but it can be done.

On the other hand, there are certain other character qualities I believe you really must have to do exceedingly well in the real estate industry. I would call them the deal breakers. The non-negotiables, that I would say if you don't have them, you're not going to make it.

Things like:

- Honesty
- Integrity
- Trustworthiness
- Reliability
- Determination
- Persistence
- Adaptability
- Creativity

If you are not already an honest person, it is not easy to become one. You can't just wave a magic wand and suddenly you're honest. If you don't have integrity, it is hard to create it. If you let people down regularly and don't do what you say you're going to do, when you say you're going to do it, that's a problem. If you're not a reliable person, people will have difficulty trusting you. But above and beyond those obvious traits, the quality of being determined is probably the next most critical to your success. It is that stick-to-it-iveness, the grit you need to persist and keep trying when the going gets tough and things aren't going your way.

When I started in the real estate business, my attitude was that failure was not an option. I was determined to figure it out. Whatever that entailed was precisely what I was going to do. My attitude was, "I will persist until I succeed." If you are not 100%, all in and determined to succeed you'll probably drop out at the first sign of trouble.

I've had a lot of determination since I was a young child. I have this strange, built-in, anti-quit mechanism that kicks in and even if I really wanted to quit, I couldn't do it. My mom liked to tell a story about the first time she noticed this when I was about five years old. I had received a pair of cross-country skis and all the gear that goes with it for Christmas that year. The problem was that I had no previous experience with skiing and no idea how to put the equipment on or how to ski properly. Unfortunately, my parents were not really much help because they had no clue. Neither of them was a skier, either.

Right after Christmas, we had a fresh snowfall and out I went, ski gear in hand, to figure it out. I quickly got frustrated trying to figure out how to get the skis on. My next challenge, once I figured that out, was how to climb what I thought was a major hill at the time. In reality, it was probably not more than two or three feet high, but it looked much bigger to a small five-year-old. I fought with those skis for hours. I kicked them around the yard. I jumped up and down, yelling and screaming. I even had a mini temper tantrum and a bit of a melt-down that day. But one thing I did not do was give up. I persisted until I succeeded. Eventually I got it.

I learned from that experience that you should never give up. Quitting is not an option. Take a break if you must but then get yourself back up, dust yourself off and push on to try again. If you persist, you will eventually succeed. Something I learned many years later is that real estate is very similar to learning how to ski: if you are 100% determined to succeed, you will.

The real estate business requires momentum. Here is a great analogy I like to use to illustrate exactly what it takes to be successful in real estate. Close your eyes and imagine a big, long, freight train. Now, imagine the longest freight train you've ever seen (with those stacked shipping containers on each car). Picture each of those shipping containers packed full of various goods (maybe even cars or big pickup trucks). Can you imagine how heavy that would be? Imagine how much weight there would be for that train engine to tow. Now, imagine that same big, long freight train (the longest one you've ever seen) with all those packed and stacked shipping containers, sitting at a standstill in the train yard. Can you imagine how much energy and effort is required to get that train moving? That train is just like a brand-new real estate representative just starting out in the real estate business. It takes a tremendous effort just to start moving. If you keep putting in the effort, working hard, doing all the right things consistently, suddenly you notice you are beginning to move. Very slowly at first. As you stick with it and continue to work very hard, you begin to pick up speed. Hey, look at you. You are going a little faster now.

Somewhere around your second year in the business, assuming you've been faithful in doing all the right things consistently, you begin to pick up more speed. Things start to get easier. You are working with a few clients now. You start putting a few deals together. Business is now starting to come to you, instead of you having to chase it all the time. You're on roll. You are flying down the tracks now. You have momentum in your business just like that big, long, freight train would have on the train tracks. Life gets easier. You can actually let up just a little on the accelerator (but not too much). You must maintain momentum at all times. If you lose it, you'll need to start all over again. Now the second time around it may come a little faster, but it is still going to take you a few months to get back on track.

Many real estate representatives fall into this trap. Just as they start to enjoy the fruits of their labor, they stop doing the daily activities that got them there in the first place. They decide they need a break. They've been working hard. They need to recharge. Besides, now that they're a successful real estate representative, they have plenty of money. There is nothing to worry about. Next year is going to be even better. They decide to go on an extended holiday to celebrate their success. Three weeks in Hawaii sounds like a really good idea. They go on the trip. They have a blast. Maybe they overindulge just a little and spend more than they anticipated. They come home after their trip and realize they now have a $10,000 credit card bill to pay off and the balance in their bank account is a little lower than they thought it should be after they paid that income tax bill and filed their HST payment.

Not to worry, they'll have a paycheck coming in soon and there is more where that came from. They are feeling a little groggy after their trip, so they need a couple of days to get back in the groove. By the time they are fully engaged and have their head in the game again, the first week back to work has passed. That's more than four weeks without focusing on those daily activities that made them successful. Guess what? They've just lost all their momentum. And unfortunately, there is no quick fix to get it back. They'll have to go back to the basics. Get back to their routine of doing those basic daily activities consistently. Day in and day out, grinding it out to fill their pipeline with potential new clients. I would say that process is probably going to take at least three-to-six months of consistency with your daily lead generation activities before your momentum fully returns and the real estate representative starts to feel good about their business again.

What is the moral of this story? In the real estate business, you must maintain your momentum once you get it going. If you lose it, you'll be starting over. Yes, it is important to celebrate your success, I am not going to argue with that. Just don't overdo it! Remember, it is usually best to do everything in moderation.

Chapter 6

The Top Five Core Competencies

There are really only a few key competencies
every great real estate representative should
have, and they are all necessary for success!
—Wayne Throop

On a typical day, real estate representatives wear many hats. You can easily find yourself leading a listing presentation or a buyer consultation meeting, doing research for clients, preparing a Comparative Market Analysis (CMA) for a potential home seller, working to generate new leads, responding to emails, showing properties to potential home buyers, negotiating offers on a property, meeting a business partner for a coffee, taking a client out for lunch, posting and responding to messages on social media, returning phone calls, creating websites, designing graphics, preparing marketing materials, updating your database, setting goals, building a business plan, taking training courses, attending office meetings, and more.

You really do need to be a bit of a Jack of all Trades to do well in this business, but you can't be a pro at everything. You must be versatile and aware of your strengths and weaknesses. The key is to play to your strengths and get help in those areas where you're not strong. Don't waste your time trying to become great at something that is simply not in your wheelhouse and doesn't come naturally to you. Yes, it is always a good idea to try to improve where you can, but I suggest you focus on getting better at the things you are already good at, actually enjoy doing, and get paid well to do. Find someone else to take care of the rest. At some point, you should plan to hire an administrative assistant to help you with all the daily tasks you don't enjoy or perhaps are not the highest and best use of your time.

If you want to become a true pro in this business, you should also plan to hire professionals to assist you with things like accounting, bookkeeping, tax returns, building and updating your website, graphic design, and producing marketing materials. You should be focusing most of your time on generating new business, finding new leads, meeting with your clients, or negotiating offers.

I suggest the following five areas are the ones most likely to contribute significantly to your long-term success:

1. Social skills

2. Communication

3. Listening

4. Technology

5. Negotiation

I recognize there is room for debate over which skills are more important than others and some might argue with the order I've chosen; I also could have included many other skills that haven't made the list. Diplomacy, for example, was very close to making my list since a great real estate representative must be very diplomatic at times and must express themselves with sensitivity. Professionalism is another prized quality in a real estate representative but it's a way of conducting oneself rather than a specific skill. I almost included research skills because it is important to stay on top of the latest stats and market trends in order to accurately assess a home's value. At the end of the day, my list of the top skills is based on my experiences as a successful real estate representative, broker manager, trainer, and business coach. I think most of the top professionals in the real estate industry would agree this is a solid list.

Let's look at each one in more detail:

1. Social Skills

There are basically two types of business a real estate agent can have. One is transactional, where the agent is like a hamster on the wheel constantly chasing after cold leads and pursuing people they don't know. The other type of business is relational. This is where a real estate representative will attract business through people they are already connected to. The problem with a transactional business is that it is purely a numbers game. It is all about the number of new leads coming in. The only way to do more business is to spend more time or money trying to attract more cold leads and running faster on that wheel. This requires a lot of time, energy, and money. I would also argue that many cold leads often prove to be more challenging to work on and tend to take much longer to result in a deal.

The best path to success in real estate is to build a relational business based on referrals from people you know, who already love and trust you. The real estate business is really a relationship business. If you are not already connected to a large sphere of influence, then you must find ways to regularly add new people to your database.

Most successful real estate agents will tell you most of their business (80% or more) comes from referrals from people with whom they already have a relationship. They invest their valuable time, energy, and money in building relationships and staying connected with people they already know. They stay connected, provide value and excellent service, they ask for the business, and they receive referrals from the people in their social network (their sphere of influence).

This is precisely why I have social skills at the top of my list. To succeed in all of the above, you have to be sociable. You have to be good at interacting with other people. You have to be a people person. That's not to say you have to be a highly extroverted, flamboyant, over-the-top, life-of-the-party kind of person everyone talks about wherever you go. In fact, that can sometimes be too much for some people and it may have the opposite effect of what you are looking for. But you also don't want to be a wallflower in the corner by yourself everywhere you go. I would suggest the best approach is to find a happy medium. For example, I don't necessarily think of myself as an outgoing, extroverted person. I would say I'm more of a "situational extrovert." By nature, I'm more of an introvert but I am very capable of becoming an extrovert when it's necessary.

I think what you'll find is that most of the time you will make the best connections with people who are like you. Focus on being the best you can be and talk to people when you are in social situations. If you are the type of person who doesn't like people, it is going to be very difficult for you to make it to the top of the real estate business.

Here is a lesson I had to learn the hard way and it may help you consider a better way to approach socializing and meeting new people. When I was a real estate salesperson, I used to love to travel to other cities to attend real estate sales conferences and training seminars. I would travel to cities all over North America, multiple times every year. Yes, I attended a lot of great real estate training sessions, I got very pumped up from all the motivational speakers, and I learned a lot of great ideas and strategies to improve my business. But my true purpose in going to these conferences and events was to network with other salespeople and build new relationships.

I learned to be very quiet around my office whenever I was going to one of these events. Often colleagues and other agents in my office would question me. Why was I going to the same event for the thirteenth time? "Haven't you already learned everything they have to say? You must know all that material inside and out by now," they would say. "Boy, you must be a slow learner!" I was very competitive in those days, and I remember snickering to myself inside thinking they just didn't get it! And that was great, I was glad they didn't, because it gave me an advantage.

The reason this gave me an advantage was that the like-minded professionals I was meeting at these events could potentially give me referral business from other cities—and I could send them business, as well. And all those nay-sayers and negative Nellies who would tell me I was wasting my time and money going to so many of these events, didn't have a clue about why I was actually going. And they knew nothing about the referral business I was getting from them. After I became skilled at networking at these events, I could normally cover the entire cost of my trip—including conference fees and a nice vacation for a few days after the event–from the income I earned through referrals I would receive from agents I met at the conferences.

Here is a key lesson I learned about networking and socializing whether at a conference or any other type of social gathering. It is more important to focus on quality over quantity.

It is far more beneficial to make deeper connections with fewer people than it is to make a lot of superficial connections with people who will not even remember who you are. When I first started going to these out-of-town conferences and events, my goal was always to meet as many people as possible. I cast a wide net. I thought that the more people I met, the better. My goal was always to come home with as many business cards as I possibly could. But then I realized that when I came home and would go through the business cards of the people I had met, I really couldn't remember who a lot of them were and I'm sure most of them wouldn't have remembered me, either. I didn't feel comfortable recommending these people to my clients and I am sure many of them felt the same way about me. There was no real connection between us. And, as I discovered, no connection usually means no business.

Over time, I learned to become more surgically precise. I began connecting with a very small number of people but built deeper, more meaningful relationships with them. Ones where we built trust and rapport. This strategy had the highest return on my investment. When I came home from a conference, I could look at the business cards of the five or six key contacts I had made, and I could safely say I knew who they were and know I would be happy to refer my clients to them. I discovered that feeling a connection with another like-minded person often leads to business. I am sure they probably felt the same way.

Being social doesn't mean you have to talk to everyone at every event you go to. It means you're good at interacting with other people and building deeper relationships with a few key people you meet. You are willing to put yourself out there and connect at a deeper level with others.

Remember it's not always about you and your business. You should approach social interactions with the intention of building relationships first and let the business take care of itself. If you come on too strong too quickly and start asking for referrals before you establish a connection, you will turn the other person off and this approach will not foster the trust and the long term, mutually beneficial, relationship you are looking for.

2. Communication Skills

Communication skills are closely related to social skills. The two go hand in hand. It is hard to be a social person if you are not a good communicator. When it comes to communication, it is important not to confuse communicating with talking. Communication is a two-way interaction between two or more people. It involves both speaking and listening. To be an effective communicator you need to be conscious of the situation and engaged with the other person. This requires active listening, reading verbal cues, and interpreting body language to make sure the people you are communicating with understand what you are trying to say. You ask them if they understand. You pay careful attention to how they respond. You repeat their responses to confirm you understand what they are saying. If you feel the other person is not understanding the point you are trying to make, you adjust and make your point in a different way until you confirm that they understand. It is also important to acknowledge them and confirm you've heard and understood what they have said.

Talking, on the other hand, is often a one-way communication where you are expressing what you want to say without actively listening to the other person. Talkers focus on what they want to say but they have very little awareness of how their message is being received or if the other person understands. They are not actively listening, nor consciously paying attention to how the other person is responding. They give little regard to what the other person is saying. They simply continue talking, trying to get their point across. Many real estate representatives are great talkers, but few are great communicators. To be a great communicator, you must be conscious of the situation and engaged with the other person. If you want to become a top real estate professional, it would be a very wise idea to focus on improving your communication skills. If you are not already a strong communicator, I would suggest you look up Toastmasters International, a well-known public speaking organization, and find a local club you can join. Trust me, it will be well worth the investment. You will be amazed by how much you can improve in just one year and if you are lucky, you might just make some new contacts that will help you grow your business at the same time.

3. Listening Skills

To be a great communicator, you must be a great listener. In fact, listening skills are as important—or possibly even more important—than your speaking skills. Remember you have two ears and one mouth. Listen twice as much as you speak. Many real estate representatives have this part backwards. They do all the talking and none of the listening.

Pay attention to the person you are communicating with. Read their body language. Watch their facial expressions. Listen carefully to watch what they say and how they say it. Ask yourself how your message is being received. Read between the lines. By actively listening to other people, you are acknowledging them and letting them know that what they have to say is important to you.

Sometimes it feels like real estate representatives are not listening because they are afraid of what they are going to hear. They believe they are too busy to engage in a long, drawn-out conversation, they just want to say what they need to say as quickly as possible, get the outcome they want, and move on to the next thing. Interestingly enough, if they were better listeners, and actually paying attention to what their clients had to say, they might just find they develop deeper and more meaningful relationships with their clients and do more business as a result.

To become the best real estate representative you can be, work on your listening skills. I would say the best real estate representatives are typically great listeners. I think you'll find there is a correlation between how well you listen, understand, and appreciate your clients, and the success you will enjoy in the real estate business.

4. Technology Skills

We're at the point in the real estate industry now where technological savviness is no longer optional; it is mandatory. Technology is advancing at an incredible pace and, like it or not, that isn't going to be changing anytime soon. In fact, it seems to me the pace of technological change is accelerating. For better or worse, the real estate industry is on the cutting edge of many of those changes. In fact, this has become so apparent that some real estate brokerages have rebranded themselves as technology companies that sell real estate.

There is no way around it: success in the real estate industry is going to require you to embrace technology. You must be willing to learn and adapt. If technology isn't one of your strengths, then you're going to need some help: hire someone who is tech savvy so they can work with you and fill in the gaps. Educate yourself by learning about technology. Take courses. Ask other professionals how they are using technology.

You don't necessarily have to be an expert on every social media platform or know exactly how to use every real estate software application available, but you do need to become comfortable with the basics. At a bare minimum, you're going to have to be comfortable checking email, uploading new listings into your MLS system, preparing legal documents electronically, uploading electronic documents to an online document storage system, obtaining digital signatures, and posting messages on social media platforms. But, as I said, that is the bare minimum. There is a whole other world of technology available to real estate representatives that many of the more successful agents are using to take their business to another level. These opportunities include videos, artificial intelligence, Virtual Office Websites (VOW), graphic design and more. If you are not using some of those newer technologies, you're very likely going to fall behind.

One technology you absolutely must embrace in your real estate career is a Customer Relationship Management (CRM) system. Industry experts have found that agents who use a CRM system to manage their business typically earn as much as 60% more than those who don't. What exactly is a CRM? And how can it benefit you? A CRM is an automated software platform that is used to store all your client relationship information and enable you to stay in touch with new leads, the contacts in your database, and the clients you are working with. You can also use it for scheduling, tracking your interactions with people, and setting reminders so you don't forget anything. It will track your daily activities and your business results. In short, it is the heartbeat of any successful long-term real estate business.

Here is an example of how you would use a CRM to benefit your business. On any given day a typical real estate agent will be in touch with many different clients, business partners, and potential new leads. All these people should be entered as contacts in your CRM. Every time you speak to one of your contacts, you enter notes into your CRM under that person's contact record to summarize what you talked about. Let's say you have a conversation with someone in June and the person mentioned they are about to become empty nesters in the fall when their youngest daughter goes to university. The next time you want to contact the same person, you would first pull up your notes and review what you talked about. You can ask them how they are enjoying being empty nesters and how their daughter is doing at university. They will appreciate your interest in how they are doing and what they have going on in their lives but, more importantly, they will appreciate that you remembered what they had told you in your previous conversation.

Or perhaps you are at a social gathering and when someone hears you are a real estate agent, they mention they are thinking of moving in about six months and they would love to talk to you about it when they are ready. What are you going to do with that information? How are you going to stay connected with that person? How are you going to remember to follow up with them at the appropriate time? A CRM makes it easy. First, make sure you have a picture of your business card on your cell phone. Then ask for their cell number so you can text it to them, so they have your contact information. Make some short notes on your phone if you can. Later, once you have time to get to a computer, you log in to your CRM system and enter any contact information you may have for the person, including their cell number—which is now on your cell phone—as well as a few notes about the conversation.

As a bonus tip here, whenever someone suggests you should follow up with them at some point in the future, I would recommend you cut the timeframe for following up in half. If someone tells you they are planning to move in about six months, you should follow up with them in three months. I have learned the hard way over the years that when someone starts talking about moving, they start thinking about it more frequently and suddenly their moving plans get accelerated. If you wait too long to reach out to them, there is a very good chance they are going to buy or sell their home with someone other than you.

Regardless of the specific technology platforms I've mentioned, the real point I am trying to make is that if you intend on succeeding at the highest possible level in the real estate business then embrace technology, rather than resist it. If you're not as tech savvy as you would like to be, surround yourself with people who are who can help you.

5. Negotiation

Buying or selling a home is a stressful and often very emotional experience for all involved. Most people don't like to negotiate with others, especially when it comes to selling their most expensive asset, their home. Unfortunately, in my case, I wouldn't say negotiation skills were my strongest asset. It wasn't something that came naturally for me and I had to work on it.

The ability to negotiate is a skill clients are willing to pay for. This is where you earn your paycheck. I hate to say it, but to become a top real estate agent, there is no way around it: you need to become a great negotiator. You will very quickly realize that negotiation in one form or another is part of everyday life in the real estate world. You'll be using your negotiation skills pretty much every day for everything from negotiating your commission, determining the listing terms and conditions, setting your listing prices, managing offers, and everything in between. The better you get at this, the more effective you will become as a real estate representative.

The good news is that your ability to effectively negotiate is a skill you can develop and get better at over time. There are a lot of great negotiation training programs available so do yourself a favor and work on this.

Becoming a great negotiator requires excellent communication and listening skills. You must be able to read a situation and understand who the key players are and how they like to be communicated with. If you can understand their communication style, you will be able to speak their language and build rapport with them, which will facilitate a much better negotiation. In a typical real estate transaction, there are often well-meaning family and friends in the background who know very little about real estate. They suddenly come out of the woodwork and start offering their advice to your clients, making the negotiation process much more complicated and difficult. This is particularly true of situations involving first time home buyers or seniors who are downsizing to a retirement home. The best way to address this is to get clear on who will be involved in helping make the final decision early in the process and get them engaged before you start negotiating.

As a real estate representative, you always need to be aware of who the key decision makers are and who the background influencers are.

Once you understand who is involved, try to assess the negotiation style of each person as best you can. Do they want things to move quickly? Would they prefer to take it slow and steady? Are they an emotional person who changes their minds with the wind? Are they a logical thinker who wants all the facts and figures to help with their decision? Are they the type of person who means exactly what they say? Perhaps they are one of those competitive people who simply has to feel like they've come out on top no matter what—they must feel like they won, and the other person lost.

Regardless of which style of negotiator you are dealing with, knowing who the key players are and how they like to negotiate will enable you to communicate more effectively and speak their language in a way they like to be spoken to. Learning to navigate the negotiation process effectively will allow you to facilitate the best possible outcome for your clients.

Chapter 7

The Next Five Things You Need to Become Good At

Success in real estate sales doesn't just happen by accident.
It is going to require skills!
—Wayne Throop

On any given day you may need to take care of a wide range of different activities to be successful in real estate but in my mind, these are the top five additional competencies you need to develop in order to make it to the top:

1. Marketing

2. Planning

3. Organizational skills

4. Creativity

5. Leadership

1. Marketing Skills

You don't necessarily need to be a marketing wizard to get into real estate, but if you want to find your way to the top of this industry, you must commit to becoming a student of marketing and learn as much about it as possible, as soon as you can. Educate yourself. Take courses. Learn from other agents. Look into what they are doing. See what's working and what's not. Pick their brains. Learn from their mistakes. The so-called "best real estate representatives" are typically the best in the business in marketing themselves to attract new clients. They are often not the best in many of the other technical aspects of the business.

According to the National Association of REALTORS® (NAR), 85% of a real estate representatives success is related to their ability to attract new business and only 15% of their success can be attributed to their technical skills. The moral of the story is that if you want to become a top real estate sales professional, you need to become very good at marketing yourself.

I recall when I was a new agent in the business, I was very naive about what it took to do exceptionally well in the real estate business. I thought I needed to have the answer to any question a client could possibly ask. I thought I had to memorize every clause in every contract, word for word and know exactly how to explain it perfectly to my clients every time. I thought I had to memorize the code of ethics and know everything there was to know about all the MLS rules. I also thought the real estate agents I saw in the glossy real estate magazines, in the newspapers, and all over the internet were the best there was.

I didn't realize that those agents were simply the best marketers. They were very successful in marketing themselves. They often presented the illusion that they were very good at what they were doing and shared the idea that everyone should want to hire them to help them buy or sell a home.

As a new agent, I was eager to learn and advance my career. I recognized there was no need to reinvent the wheel.

My strategy was simple. I watched what the successful agents were doing, and I would copy them, doing it in my own style.

I looked up to some of these "top agents." They were my role models. I used to question whether I could ever get to their level. But then the more I started to work with some of these agents, the more I realized that many of them were not as great as I thought they were. In fact, some of them were not very good at all. They were just great marketers. They were very good at selling the illusion that they were a superstar agent... and people were buying it.

I'd be willing to bet that if I asked you to do some research and come back and tell me who the top ten real estate representatives are in your city, the names you provided would all be the best in the business of marketing themselves. They would likely be the highest income earners, but they would not necessarily be the best overall agents in terms of their knowledge or expertise, or the level of service they provided to their clients. A real estate representative's income or the number of awards they have received does not always accurately reflect the quality of the services they provide.

The real key to sustainable, long-term success in the real estate industry, is to be great at what you do, provide exceptional service to your clients and be a great marketer to spread the word about you and your business so you are always attracting a steady stream of new clients.

2. Planning

It has been said that failing to plan is the same thing as planning to fail. You simply cannot succeed at a high level in the real estate business if you are flying by the seat of your pants with no real plan to get where you want to go. Success doesn't just happen by accident. It requires thorough planning and execution. Now, maybe you don't see yourself as a big planner, but I would suggest that if planning is not something you are naturally good at, then work on it. There are a lot of great books on planning that you can read. Take some training or listen to some podcasts. Do whatever you need to do but take the time to educate yourself and improve your planning skills.

You might be surprised to know you are probably already a better planner than you realize. Think about planning a trip to Hawaii for example. Here is how easy it would be to plan your trip:

1.   You determine your budget for the trip.
2.   You confirm you are able to take the time off for your vacation.
3.   You decide on the date you'd like to arrive and the date you'd like to return home.
4.   You decide where you'd like to stay while you are in Hawaii.
5.   You go on-line and research the flight and hotel options.
6.   You check availability and pricing for your flights to and from Hawaii.
7.   You choose the best flight options that fit your budget, and you book your tickets.
8.   You compare resorts and hotels and decide on the best option that fits your budget.
9.   You book your hotel for your stay.
10. You book the shuttle bus to take you from the airport to your resort.
11. You research all the great activities and adventures you can enjoy while you are in Hawaii.
12. You buy new luggage a week before you go.

13. The day before you go you pack your bags.

And so on. You get the idea. Well, achieving success in real estate is no different than planning a nice vacation. You decide where you'd like to go. You decide when you'd like to get there. Then you come up with the exact steps you need to take to make it happen. There is your plan! It is as simple as that. Don't overthink it. Planning a road map to your success really isn't complicated. Determine what your goals are and then what action steps you need to take to achieve those goals. But at the end of the day, if you just can't become a proficient planner, then get some help from someone who is. A great book I would recommend to help get you started is *7 Habits of Highly Effective People: Powerful Lessons in Personal Change* by Stephen R. Covey.

3. Organizational Skills

You may not necessarily consider yourself to be the most organized person by nature, but this is an area you absolutely must work on improving if you have any hope of climbing to the top of the real estate industry. As your business grows and you start to climb your way up the real estate ladder, you are going to have to become increasingly organized so you can use your time effectively. You must always be conscious of how you are using your time and make sure you are focusing on those highly productive tasks which are the highest and best use of your time.

And you should always play to your strengths. As I mentioned earlier, you need to focus on the things you are very good at that are revenue-generating activities and delegate the rest. Surround yourself with key people who can help with the day-to-day administrative activities while you focus most of your time on connecting and networking with other like-minded people, generating new business, meeting with clients, showing properties, negotiating offers and closing deals.

The best way to stay organized is to create and implement systems you use consistently to run your business. A system is basically just a documented series of steps you are going to follow consistently every time you do something. To become a successful real estate agent, you should create systems for any repetitive tasks you perform regularly.

This would include things like:

- Managing and tracking your interactions with clients using a Customer Relationship Management (CRM) system
- Lead generation, follow-up, and conversion following one of the many lead generation systems available
- Managing your listings using a listing checklist to ensure consistent services
- Working with buyers to help them purchase a home using a specific set of steps you follow consistently every time
- Establishing a specific formula for open houses you follow every time you do one
- Creating a standardized process for making an offer on a property
- Processing a transaction and uploading all your documentation to an electronic document storage system
- Post-sale stay-in-touch systems where you stay in contact with your clients in a systematic way

- Business tracking that allows you to keep track of your daily lead generation activities, new leads, sales, average sale price, commission percentage etc.
- Expense tracking using an electronic accounting system and producing monthly profit and loss reports

The more systemized your business becomes, the more efficient and effective you will be as a real estate professional and the more income you are likely to earn.

4. Creativity

Remember that the real estate business, like most other businesses, is constantly changing. Everyone seems to be out to change the way people buy and sell homes. New technologies are introduced. Industry disruptors with new business models appear almost overnight and disappear just as quickly. Every day seems to present new challenges which need to be addressed. If you like variety, then the real estate business is a good fit for you. No two days are ever the same. Just when you thought you'd seen everything, something new pops up you never would have imagined could be possible. This constantly changing environment is going to require you to be creative, to find solutions to help your clients navigate this ever-changing business.

If you're not already a creative person you might wonder how you can become one. The good news is, you can improve and get better through practice. Creativity is not about perfection, it is about getting curious, experimenting. Trying different things. Looking at a challenge from different angles. Brainstorming ideas with others. If you want to work on your creativity, I'm happy to share a little exercise I came up with. This works for me and maybe you'll find it helpful too.

Take a moment to think of a challenge you would like to overcome. Make time to sit down in a quiet place where you won't be disturbed and write about your challenge in a journal. Describe the situation in detail. Isolate the specific problem you'd like to solve. Then just start writing out possible solutions you can think of to solve that problem. Get curious about it. Write down everything that comes to mind no matter how ridiculous it might seem. It is not necessary to be realistic at this point. Just write everything down. The key is to keep going after each solution you come up with. Repeatedly ask yourself "what else?" When you first start doing this, you'll find yourself wanting to give up after three or four ideas. You have to press on and keep going. Write out as many ideas as you can in about thirty minutes. Then take a break for ten minutes. Come back and ask yourself the same question again. I think you'll find new ideas and possible solutions will come up during your second attempt. And when you think you've exhausted all possibilities, ask yourself again, "is there anything else?" If you are dealing with a particularly difficult challenge you may need to repeat this process multiple times.

Once you have an exhaustive list, scan through your ideas and eliminate the ones which obviously won't work and keep doing this until you are left with a very short list of just a couple of ideas you want to try out. I find this helpful, so give it a try if you want to become more creative.

Cultivating creativity is like building body muscle. It takes time and consistent effort to produce the results you want. Creativity is no different. If you want to become a more creative person, practice and put in the effort to improve. And with everything changing and new challenges coming up daily, your creativity is more important than ever when serving your clients. More importantly for real estate representatives is that this is a skill people will pay for. As the business continues to evolve, real estate representatives are going to have to rely on their creativity to continue to thrive and succeed at the highest level in the real estate industry.

5. Leadership

I believe the world is starving for great leaders to step forward. Real estate is no exception. Every real estate transaction requires leadership. Every client, whether they realize it or not, needs a good leader to guide them successfully through the process of buying or selling real estate. A great leader will motivate their clients to achieve their real estate goals. In many cases, being a great leader in the real estate industry means protecting clients from themselves. They are often their own worst enemy and, unfortunately, they can unknowingly cost themselves thousands of dollars. There is an expression I often refer to in the real estate business:

If you want to frustrate a client, let them get their own way.

It's tempting for homeowners to think they can save the cost of paying the real estate commission fees—thereby putting more money in their own pockets–by buying or selling a home privately on their own. Typically, this proves to be a very expensive decision and over the years, I've seen many people cost themselves hundreds of thousands of dollars going this route... and they don't even realize it happened.

Here is a story about what often happens when people buy or sell their homes privately. As a real estate agent, a significant amount of my business came through referrals I received from my network of business connections. One of these contacts was a financial planner. He called me up one day and said "I have a great referral for you. I've recommended you to clients of mine, a young couple, who are planning to purchase their first home. The good news for you is that they've already found the home they'd like to buy. All you have to do is go show them the home and do up the paperwork."

Wow, this sounded too good to be true, but I was excited to hear from them and help them navigate the purchase process. He said, "they should be calling you shortly." I eagerly waited for their call, but my phone didn't ring. That afternoon and evening came and went with no call. The next day came and went, and I still hadn't heard from them. Finally, a day later, I called the person who had given me the referral and I told him I still hadn't heard from his clients. He said, "let me give them a call and I will get back to you."

He called me a couple of hours later with the bad news. It turns out those young, naive, misinformed, first-time home buyers thought they could save themselves some money, so they had gone ahead and purchased a home being sold privately on their own without an agent.

The house had been listed for sale at $350,000 and they thought that if they didn't have an agent, they would save the 2.5% commission fee they thought they were going to have to pay one, so they offered the seller the full asking price. In that buyer's mind, they thought they were saving $8,750 by not working with an agent; they figured it was fine to go ahead and pay the full price the private seller was asking for the home. They didn't understand that it is typically the sellers who pay the commission, not the buyers. All they had to do was talk to me first, and I could have explained everything to them.

After I heard which home they had purchased, I went and did my research and determined that its actual market value was not more than $325,000. If they had worked with me as their real estate agent, they would not have paid a penny more than that, so they overpaid for the home by $25,000 just to "save" $8,750. And they don't even realize how much money they lost in the transaction. Like I said, people who are buying or selling real estate need a trusted adviser, a great leader to help them through the process.

Here is another example of clients erroneously thinking they're going to save a few dollars by leaning into their own independence. It started off when I advised a couple not to purchase an overpriced home which was being sold privately. They bought it anyway, overpaying by at least $50,000 in an area that wasn't very nice. A few months later, they realized their mistake and they recognized they should have listened to my advice. They decided to move, but because they were embarrassed by not listening to my advice in the first place, they decided to sell privately to try and recoup some of the money they had lost by overpaying for the home they bought. They overpriced their home when they were trying to sell it so, unfortunately, there were no buyers interested in buying it.

While it was still on the market, they made another mistake when they decided to again purchase another overpriced home that was listed for sale privately. This time they overpaid by $75,000 with an unconditional offer to purchase their new home in the country. Remember, rural properties typically have wells and septic systems. Unfortunately, because they had no professional agent representing their best interests, they were not protected. They had no condition in their offer to purchase regarding the sale of their existing home, nor did they include a condition for either the inspection of the home or the septic system.

It turned out that their old home had not sold by the time they had to close the deal to purchase their new home, so they had to drop their price $50,000 below what they had paid in order to sell it. To further complicate this situation, it turned out after they moved into the new place, the property they purchased had structural issues and the septic system was shot and needed to be replaced at an additional cost of more than $30,000. This whole situation had become a comedy of errors.

If you do the math, these people cost themselves more than $150,000 by trying to save the money they were going to have to pay a real estate representative for their commission fees... which would have been less than $40,000.

Like I said, if you want to frustrate a client let them get their own way. When it comes to buying or selling a home, everyone needs a great professional to help lead them through the process.

PART 2

WHAT YOU NEED
(TECHNOLOGY AND RESOURCES)

Chapter 8

You Are Running a Business

*Make no mistake: when you start a career as
an independent real estate agent working on
your own, you are starting a business.*
—Wayne Throop

Congratulations! You are now the Chief Executive Officer (CEO) of your very own company. Oh, and you are also now the Chief Operating Officer (COO) and the Chief Financial Officer (CFO). You'll be wearing all three hats if you plan to be successful in this business. Although you may work for a real estate brokerage, in most cases you will be an independent contractor operating as a sole proprietor or, if you are successful in your career, perhaps as a Personal Real Estate Corporation (PREC).

Most people who get into the real estate business must make a mindset shift in order to think of themselves as a business owner. You are not just "in" the real estate business, you now "have" a real estate business. You are not just earning a paycheck by helping people buy and sell real estate; you are running a business that helps people buy and sell real estate and in addition to selling homes, you have income to track, expenses to pay, marketing and business plans to create, goals to set... and don't forget about creating and managing systems to keep your business running smoothly. There is a whole lot more to it than simply helping people buy and sell homes.

I've heard it said that most real estate professionals aim for nothing and hit it with amazing accuracy! That is so true!

Did you know that some industry experts suggest that fewer than 3% of all real estate agents have a written business plan? I find that hard to believe: I thought it would be less than that. If you think about it, if you don't know where you want to go, and you don't have a plan to go anywhere, you're probably just going to spin your wheels and keep going around in circles. You're probably going to be spending time and money doing things that aren't going to produce the results that will lead you to success. And, if you are one of the few people with a written goal of stating where they'd like to go, how could you possibly be successful if you don't have a plan to get there?

What would you do if you were sitting in New York City and wanted to drive to Vancouver? In the old days, you probably would have pulled out a map and planned your route. Things are significantly easier today now that we have GPS technology. But you still must decide which route you will take and where you'd like to stop along the way. You must plan how long you will drive each day and pick the cities where you would like to stay each night. You must decide on a budget, book the hotels where you are planning to stay, and then decide what you will do when you arrive in Vancouver. In other words, you must come up with a plan to get from where you are to where you want to be. Why wouldn't real estate professionals do the same?

The problem I see with many real estate agents is that they don't have clear written goals that specifically define exactly what they want to achieve They may have some vague notion of selling twenty homes or earning $150,000 next year but they really don't know why, nor do they have any real plan to get there. Certainly not a written one. In fact, many agents also don't know exactly where they're "at" with business either, so they have no real starting point. If you don't know where you are starting from it becomes extremely difficult to come up with a plan to get you where you want to be. If you have any intention of succeeding at the highest levels in this business, you're going to need a concrete plan to get there. It is not going to just happen by accident. If you are doing the right things consistently, for an extended period, good things are going to happen.

Agents can choose from plenty of great training programs to learn in greater detail exactly what they need to do to have a successful real estate sales business but at a high level, here are the concrete steps you should start with:

1. Determine exactly where your business is today by reviewing your past results:

a. How many sales have you done in the past twelve months?

b. What is the average sale price of the homes you've sold?

c. What is the average commission you earn on each sale?

d. How many leads do you need to end up with one transaction?

e. How many contacts do you have to make to generate a new lead?

f. How many days do you work in a week?

g. How many weeks do you work in a year?

If you know these numbers, you can figure out exactly what you must do daily to achieve your goals for the year. If you are new to the business, just estimate what you'd like to see happen over the next twelve months and then keep track of your numbers as the year unfolds. You may find you must adjust your expectations depending on how things go.

2. **Determine exactly where you want to go and put it in writing (be very specific about what it is and when you'd like to do it). Think about creating SMART goals (they are Specific, Measurable, Achievable, Realistic, and Time-based).**

   a.   How much income do you want to earn in the next twelve months?
   b.   How many homes do you want to sell?
   c.   How many days would you like to work every week?
   d.   How many weeks would you like to take off next year?

3. **Create an action plan by laying out the specific steps you will take to achieve your goals.**

4. **Determine what specific activities you are going to do daily to generate new leads.**

   a.   Calling past and current clients
   b.   Texting
   c.   Sending Emails
   d.   Sending videos
   e.   Writing personal notes
   f.   Social media interactions (like, comment, share, post)
   g.   Monthly newsletters
   h.   Email drip campaigns
   i.   Coffee meetings
   j.   Lunch meetings
   k.   Business networking

l.   Client parties
m. Open houses
n.   Content Marketing
o.   Websites/online leads
p.   Geographic farming
q.   Community involvement

Regardless of which lead generation strategies you choose to focus on, many real estate business coaches agree agents should aim for about three touches every month or about thirty-to-sixty touches per year with each person in your database. I know you're probably thinking that sounds like a lot, but keep in mind this includes any combination of the strategies listed above. Here is an example of how easy this could be. You send a monthly newsletter to your contacts, connect with them on social media by liking a picture they posted and add a comment, you give them a quick phone call and arrange to meet them for a coffee. Just like that, you've had four touches with the same person in less than thirty days.

Here is what a simple business plan might look like for a typical real estate representative:

Let's say your goal is to earn $200,000 in gross commission in the next year.

You've determined that over the past twelve months your average gross commission for every home you sold was $10,000 per transaction. Based on those numbers, you will need to do twenty transactions to achieve your commission goal for next year.

Let's take it a step further and assume you plan to work four days a week and take two weeks off, so you'll be working fifty weeks for a total of 200 days next year. If you break that down to ten hours per day x 200 days that equals 2,000 hours. If you take $200,000 and divide it by 2,000 hours that translates into an hourly rate of $100/hour.

If you have a system for tracking your daily activities and results, you know exactly which activities will generate the results you want. Let's say your tracking shows you can complete one sale for every five leads (the actual number may fluctuate due to market changes). Let's say you have also determined that ten contacts result in one new lead. That means that for every fifty contacts you make, you'll complete one sale. So, if your goal is to do twenty transactions, the math looks like this:

50 contacts x 20 transactions = 1,000 contacts

If you take those 1,000 contacts and divide them by the 200 days you are planning to work next year, that would mean you need to make five contacts every day. One contact every two hours. Now you know that if you make those five contacts consistently every working day over the next year, you can safely predict you will achieve your income goal.

Let's look at this from a different angle: if you're planning to work forty hours a week and you are taking two weeks for vacation, that means you'll work approximately 2,000 hours in a year. As we've seen, if your goal is to earn $200,000, then you must earn $100 per hour. Assess everything you do on an hourly basis from this perspective and ask yourself if what you are doing is worth $100 an hour. If you could pay someone else less than $100 an hour to do that task, you should be delegating the job to someone else and focusing your attention on those high-dollar activities that are earning you the most money. Always ask yourself whether what you are doing is the highest and best use of your time.

The key to being able to create a meaningful business plan is to track your daily activities and results on a consistent basis. This enables you to predict with almost 100% certainty precisely what you must do every working day to achieve your goals. Wouldn't that feel great?

My advice would be to keep it simple when you get started with your business plan. There is no need to overcomplicate this the first few times you do it.

5. Create budgets for both your business and personal expenses. (And don't be afraid to invest in yourself).

One thing I'd like to point out is that you are running a business, and you need to invest time and money in it. One mistake I see many real estate professionals making is that they starve their business by not investing sufficient money in developing themselves or it. They see it as an expense rather than an investment.

One of the best ways to grow your real estate business is to invest in yourself. Focus on becoming the best version of yourself possible. Go to seminars and conferences. Take regular training classes. Learn from successful colleagues. Read personal development books. If you see an opportunity to learn, grow, and improve your skills, take it! The better you get, the more value you can offer your clients and the more income you will attract. The best investment you can ever make is in yourself. It offers the best returns and the knowledge and skills you acquire can never be taken away from you. If you plan to be successful in the real estate business, you simply must set aside some money in your budget for personal growth and development.

As a guideline, for a solo real estate agent working on their own, you should anticipate spending between 25%-35% of your gross income on your business expenses. I would say at least 5% of that should be allocated towards your personal development. Expenses for a real estate team will likely run closer to 50%-to-60% of your gross income. But between 5% and 10% of that should be spent on personal growth and development for the members of your team.

One of the best ways to learn, grow, and become a better version of yourself is to learn from the pros. Learn what the more successful agents are doing and then implement their ideas in your own business. Look around and figure out who the successful agents are. As a rule, most of them are generally happy to help. Invite them out for a coffee or lunch. Ask them if you can pick their brains to get some ideas. Yes, their lunch will cost you a few dollars, but this is a very small price to pay for the advice and ideas you are going to receive during that meeting. It might just give you the one idea that could double your business next year.

Here is a story I'd like to share with you that relates to the courageous decision I made to invest in myself when I was new to the real estate business. At the end of my first year in the business, I was struggling and feeling frustrated, but I wasn't going to give up. I started watching the more experienced people and tried to understand what they were doing that was leading to their success. I noticed that most of the more successful agents in my brokerage were going to a particular real estate conference in Toronto. I decided there must be something to that conference and perhaps I should also go. But there was one small problem: I had no money. I was broke and couldn't afford to go. (Or at least that's what I thought.)

After a few interesting conversations with my wife, I was able to scratch together enough money to go to the conference.

I was going on a shoestring budget, so I had to share a hotel room with a colleague, which turned out to be a disaster. He had a very bad snoring problem. After four frustrating hours of tossing and turning while trying to fall asleep, I couldn't take it any longer. I went down to the front desk to try and get another room for myself. I told them if they couldn't find me a room, I was prepared to sleep on the couch in the hotel lobby because it would probably be quieter than my hotel room. Fortunately, they found me a room and I was able to get some much-needed rest. (Thank you, credit card!)

The next day I learned why so many of the great agents from our brokerage were attending the conference. It was fantastic. I learned a lot about the importance of personal growth and how it could benefit my business. I was hooked! As the conference went on, organizers began talking about one-on-one business coaching and noted that many real estate agents had doubled and tripled their business by signing up for a business coaching program. I quickly realized that this was exactly what I needed to do. Oh, but wait, remember I had no money at the time?

Only $7,000 a Year!

I was totally pumped and excited about it when I called my wife at the break and told her this was exactly what I needed to do. She was less excited about the idea than I was and did not share any of my enthusiasm. In fact, she became downright annoyed when I told her it was only $7,000 for a whole year. I am pretty sure her exact words were "Absolutely not, you can't afford that! You have no money, remember?" I was disappointed but realized she was probably right. On the last day of the conference, the speaker was again talking about the business coaching they offered and how it could improve my business and increase my income. He was a very good salesperson and the more I heard him talk about it the more I knew I just had to do this.

Finally, I had a breakthrough. I had an amazing idea: I could use the line of credit my wife and I had! I made my decision. I called my wife and with 100% conviction I told her this was what I was doing. I bit the bullet and signed up. I paid my $7,000 and I hired a business coach for the next twelve months of my life. I reassured my wife that this was the best thing for me to do and that I was totally responsible for the $7,000 on our line of credit.

They say fate rewards the courageous and it turned out to be true in this case. I made that courageous decision and guess what? I was super motivated to do everything my coach told me to do because I just knew failure was not an option. I would never hear the end of it if I failed. The next year, I increased my sales from nine deals to thirty-four deals. I had made a $7,000 investment and earned more than $140,000 in additional income during that twelve-month period.

I am not suggesting everyone should make the same decision I did but the point I want to make here is that you really need to invest in yourself. Absolutely, you should go to the conferences, take the training, read the books, take the pros out for lunch and, yes, spend the money to learn and grow as a person. Develop yourself and learn ways to bring more value to your clients. Your income will grow in direct proportion to the amount you grow and improve as a person.

Chapter 9

What You Need to Have
in Order to Succeed

Investing in yourself always offers the highest rate of return!
—Wayne Throop

A lot of ingredients can go into creating a successful real estate business, but I feel a certain few are mandatory. You might feel like I'm stating the obvious here but believe it or not there is a reason I'm including it: you are going to need a reliable car to drive if you plan to be successful in real estate. You don't necessarily have to drive a high-end luxury car, but you should have a decent car suitable for driving a client to see a house. I've only heard of one person who was somehow able to create success without a car (or a driver's license). But the other 99.99% of real estate agents are going to need a car and license to drive to be successful. Can you imagine a real estate representative trying to explain to a client they don't actually have a car or a driver's license? You are also going to need money to put gas in your car and maintain it.

That means that you will need both a personal budget and a business budget. It is critical that you know exactly where you are spending your money and how much you need to earn monthly to cover your basic fixed costs. One of the more common mistakes I see many real estate salespeople make is that they overspend on their personal expenses and then starve their business, refusing to invest in things they need to build a successful business. As a real estate professional, you are a self-employed business owner, and you must think like one. Set aside a reasonable amount of money for business expenses.

At the beginning of your real estate career, you may need to sacrifice on some of your discretionary personal expenses to fund your business. But let that motivate rather than discourage you. Make those sacrifices early in your career, build your business, earn the money, build up your financial reserves, and then, once you've achieved financial stability, go spend the surplus on a luxury car or exotic vacation. Just do it in that order. I've seen way too many real estate representatives spend money on their personal lifestyle before they have stability in their business and enough of a reserve fund to carry them through difficult times. Realistically, when you start your real estate business your reserve fund should contain enough cash to pay your start-up costs, as well as your business and personal expenses for at least the first six months (twelve months would be even better).

Did you know that according to the National Association of REALTORS® (NAR), the average real estate agent in the United States earns less than $10,000 in their first year in the business? It is extremely difficult to get started, and you don't need the added financial stress of not having enough money to pay your bills at the same time. Some brokerages will cover a good portion of your start-up costs but you're still going to incur some expenses, and you are going to be paying all your personal expenses during that difficult time when you really don't have much income coming in.

Basic Start-up Costs for a New Real Estate Agent

Although the exact costs will vary depending on your jurisdiction and real estate brokerage, typical start-up costs for a new real estate agent in their first two years in the business might look something like the following:

1. Pre-license Education $3,500-$4,000 (one time).
2. License/Registration $350-$400 (one time).
3. Errors and Omissions Insurance $500 (annually).
4. Registration and Initiation fees for Professional Associations $1,400-$1,500 (one time).
5. Real Estate Board Fees $1,800 (annually).
6. Additional Real Estate Association fees $500 (annually).
7. Post-Registration Education $600 (one time).
8. Real Estate Company Corporate Fees $2,000-$3,200 (annually).

Year One Total: Approximately $10,000
Year Two Total: Approximately $6,500

It is important to keep in mind that these expenses are just the basic minimum expenses required before you can call yourself a licensed real estate salesperson. They do not include any of your operating expenses for your business such as gas and maintenance for your vehicle, your technology expenses such as your cell phone, laptops, or tablets, etc. And don't forget about your marketing expenses, administration costs, bookkeeping, and accounting expenses. Realistically, you should anticipate spending at least $1,200-$1,500 per month just to be in the business, and this number could be significantly greater.

Not to discourage anyone, but you should also anticipate going at least six months without a paycheck and even that might be optimistic for some. Take your monthly business and personal expenses combined (let's say a minimum of $3,500), multiply by six months, and you'll need to have at least $21,000 available to get started. You must ask yourself if you are able to do that.

Depending on your business plan and your personal lifestyle, you could certainly spend a lot more than that. Many agents who are new to the business are transitioning into real estate from another career or working a part-time job somewhere else to help pay the bills. This might be feasible for a short period of time, but it won't work in the long run. Whenever someone asks me if working in another job full time while starting a new career in real estate will work, I tell them, "if you chase two rabbits, they both get away!" Real estate is hard enough on its own without trying to juggle another job at the same time.

The next thing you are going to need is an office. Regardless of whether you are planning to work in an office provided by your brokerage or work from home, real estate is a very mobile business, and you are going to need home office space with good internet service for those after-hours real estate tasks that are bound to come up at some point. There is nothing more frustrating than trying to get a document signed under a tight timeline while dealing with a poor internet connection at your home office (trust me, I've been there).

Make Friends with Technology

I am not going to candy-coat this next point just to make you feel better. I'd rather give you an honest assessment of what this business is really like behind the scenes so you can understand what it is going to take to make it. You might as well face reality. As I mentioned earlier, if you're to have any hope of succeeding in the real estate business, you must get comfortable using technology. Real estate has become a high-tech business, and your success will require some basic tech equipment such as a smartphone, a reliable computer such as a laptop, desktop computer, or tablet, and a decent printer. You don't need the latest and greatest version of each, but they certainly do need to be reliable.

In addition to the hardware, you are going to need some reliable software applications to manage your business. This will include a Customer Relationship Management (CRM) system, an email application, some form of online calendar, and an electronic document storage system, to name a few. The bottom line here is that you must feel comfortable using at least the basics of technology, otherwise you are going to need some help.

You will also need training, mentoring, and coaching. You are going to need a significant amount of help that goes way above and beyond the material you cover in your real estate licensing program in order to be successful in real estate. Now, a word of caution here: not all brokerages are equal when it comes to the training and support they offer and there can be significant differences between them in this area. Making the wrong choice when deciding which brokerage to join can, in many cases, mean the difference between success and failure. Choose carefully. Do your homework and make sure you are clear on what is being offered.

You might say I'm a little biased in my next suggestion considering I am a real estate business coach but I'm going to say it anyway: I firmly believe every real estate professional should have a coach or mentor of some kind. Think about it. What do all professional athletes have in common? They all have a coach! If you want to succeed at the highest levels in the real estate business, you're going to need some coaching to get there. A good coach has a way of drawing out the best in you. They will help you become the best version of yourself possible. Honestly, a coach will require you to do a lot of hard work and heavy lifting. Their job is to support and encourage you, hold you accountable for the things you commit to doing, and help guide you in creating an action plan to work towards achieving your goals. The coach doesn't do everything for you. They guide you in discovering how to do it yourself.

I would say hiring a business coach is a no-brainer. Yes, some brokerages offer in-house business coaching for free, or possibly a nominal monthly fee, but, in most cases, coaching is going to require you to make a financial investment. But, as I said before, the best investment anyone can ever make is in themselves. It is always the investment with the greatest rate of return. The cost of hiring a coach varies quite a bit but you can probably anticipate $500-$1,500 per month depending on who you choose to work with. Nevertheless, regardless of the investment required, it is going to be money very well spent. Think about it. If you worked diligently with a coach for one solid year, don't you think you could do at least two extra sales as a result? If your average commission was around $10,000 that would mean $20,000 over and above what you otherwise would have made. Even if you only did those two extra deals, that is still a great return on your investment.

My guess is that if you put in the hard work and were diligent in completing the action steps you agreed to with your coach, you could do five or more deals above and beyond what you would have otherwise done and even that might be a conservative number. And that is just in your first year. Imagine how much that would amount to over an entire career! When I first hired a coach, my sales went from nine deals one year to thirty-four deals the following year. Those extra twenty-five deals I closed covered the cost of my coaching and then some! Like I said, working with a reputable coach should be a no-brainer for any real estate salesperson. Think of it as an investment in your business. You might not think you can afford it, which is how I felt at first, too. But the truth is, you can't afford not to. Success requires coaching. And where there is a will, there's a way! Make the decision and you'll find the money!

Chapter 10

Your Support Network

If you want to go fast, go alone.
If you want to go far, go together!
—African Proverb

If you ask anyone who has achieved a high level of success in the real estate business, they will all tell you they couldn't have done it alone. In the wild, it is said that a predator never attacks the pack, they always go after the lone straggler, the one that's off on their own. Don't be the Lone Ranger, off doing your own thing flying solo all the time. This is very likely to leave you feeling lonely and isolated, and you won't enjoy what you are doing. In addition, you'll probably find it very frustrating and not very profitable.

Many business coaches will tell you that business success hinges on relationships but there is probably no industry where this is truer than in the real estate business. Strong connections with supportive, like-minded people who are big advocates of you and your business are key to success in real estate. The raving fans who bang the drums and tell the world how great you are, and let the world know that anyone who is moving should be using your services. These are the key people who you need to be working hard to stay in touch with, deepening your relationships with them, and building their confidence and trust in you so they will feel confident in referring you to their family members and friends.

Regardless of where you are working, find your tribe and surround yourself with like-minded, growth-oriented people who are pushing you to achieve *more*. I would suggest that if you are the smartest person in the room, you are in the wrong room. Surround yourself with people who are smarter than you are, who will challenge you and who are already at the level you aspire to reach. I've read somewhere you will earn the average income of the five people you spend the most time with. So, look around. Who are you spending most of your time with? What would their average income be? Are these people succeeding at the level you'd like to reach? Honestly, now, are these people challenging you to grow? Do they have a positive attitude? Do they support and encourage you? If not, maybe it is time to look for new people to hang out with.

A good way to find your tribe is to join a mastermind group. If there isn't one already available to you to join, then start a new one. You might be asking yourself what exactly a mastermind group is. Simply put, it is a group of peers who meet regularly to encourage each other, brainstorm ideas, find solutions to common challenges, and offer advice and support for the benefit of each member. There is absolutely no need to go it alone in this business. The shortest and best path to success is always found through the support and encouragement of others who are heading in the same direction you want to go. After finding a good coach, the next best thing you can do is to find your tribe and form a mastermind group!

Another one of the next best things anyone can do to succeed in the real estate business is to find yourself a good mentor. Most brokerages will encourage this and some even offer formal mentoring programs to newer agents. When you are first starting out there is a lot to learn on the road to success. Why not find yourself a real pro who's already been successful and learn from them? They can be your cheerleader,

114

encouraging you when the going gets tough (which it will). Where do you find a great mentor? Look around your brokerage and find someone you think would make a good role model— someone who has a business you'd like to emulate—and ask them if they would consider mentoring you.

Be prepared to work hard as you're likely going to get stuck doing a lot of their grunt work, but that's how it works. That's how you learn. Chances are you will need to find your own leads, and then bring your mentor in to help you through the process, but don't expect them to do it for free. That is not realistic. It is very likely they will expect to split any commissions you may earn from your deals 50-50 or maybe, if you are lucky, they would be willing to settle for 25%. Either way, don't get cheap here. They are giving up their valuable time, energy, and expertise to help you learn how to thrive in the business. I would say that regardless of what they charge, this is one of the best investments you can make to uplevel your business much quicker. The advice and guidance you will receive will be worth its weight in gold and I'm confident you will agree it is money very well spent.

A Word on Networking

The road to success doesn't end here though. Yes, having a great coach, being a part of a mastermind group of like-minded peers and having great mentors within your brokerage are going to accelerate your journey towards success but there is a lot more you can do outside of your brokerage to build your business. Networking with other business owners outside of real estate can be hugely beneficial in growing your business, as well. Consider establishing a network of like-minded small business owners, contractors, tradespeople, real estate lawyers, mortgage advisors, and other professionals to connect with. Get to know them and their businesses better, so you can create a reliable network of qualified professionals you can trust and to whom you can refer your clients. And from what I've learned, when you help someone else build their business, they almost always reciprocate and want to help you build yours.

So, where do you find these people? The opportunities are endless. You can join your local Community Association, Chamber of Commerce, Business Improvement Association (BIA), other local clubs like the Rotary Club, Kiwanis Club, a golf club or a curling club or, if you prefer online options, you could join some appropriate LinkedIn or Facebook groups. Join any club or organization where you can connect with other business professionals from your community.

I suggest the best thing to do would be to either join an existing business networking group or start a new one. Joining an established group, like Business Networking International (BNI), might be easier if you can find one with an open spot for a real estate representative. These groups are made up of business professionals from a variety of different fields who meet on a regular basis to help each other build their businesses through referrals between members. Typically, these groups only allow one member from each profession and there is a lot of competition for the real estate seat so it can be a challenge to find a group with a vacancy. This can be a great opportunity to make some amazing connections and increase your sales.

I have been a member of a business networking group in one form or another for my entire real estate career. Over the years, I would say this has probably been the biggest single source of income for my entire real estate business. In my most productive year, I sold more than $10,000,000 dollars' worth of real estate through referrals I received from my business partners. The networking groups I've been a part of typically meet for breakfast once a week for about an hour. Yes, it has cost money to join and pay for my breakfasts, but this has proven to be one of the most profitable ways to generate new business consistently. Again, my best advice is to not be afraid to invest in your business. Spend the money and join a business networking group. If you can't find one to join, start a new one!

PART 3

WHAT YOU DO
(SYSTEMS, BEHAVIORS,
AND HABITS)

Chapter 11

Staying Organized and Being Productive

Being organized is one of the best ways to use your time efficiently and increase your productivity!
—Wayne Throop

One thing we can all agree on is that everyone has the same amount of time to work with each week. We all have twenty-four hours in a day and there are seven days in a week. The only difference between the person earning $35,000 per year and the person earning $1,000,000 lies in what they do with their time. You don't have to work seventy to eighty hours a week and drive yourself into the ground, sacrificing your health and personal relationships to be successful in the real estate business. Simply learn to use your time wisely. Get yourself into a consistent daily routine.

I recommend you create a time-blocked calendar to guide your daily use of time. Realistically, you won't be able to follow it perfectly, but, even if you can follow it 75% of the time, you'll be far more productive than most people and you will feel much more in control of your schedule.

Sample time blocked schedule:

Sample Time Blocked Schedule

Time	Monday	Tuesday	Wednesday	Thrusday	Friday	Saturday	Sunday
6:00 AM							
6:30 AM	Morning routine	Morning routine	Morning routine	Morning routine	Morning routine	Sleep In	Sleep In
7:00 AM							
7:30 AM							
8:00 AM	Breakfast	Breakfast	Breakfast	Breakfast	Business Networking Group		
8:30 AM	Flexible	Flexible	Flexible	Flexible		Morning routine	Morning routine
9:00 AM	Lead Generation Activities	Lead Generation Activities	Lead Generation Activities	Lead Generation Activities			
9:30 AM							
10:00 AM							
10:30 AM	Return calls / reply to emails	Training & Personal Development	Return calls / reply to emails	Return calls / reply to emails	Weekly Check in with all clients		
11:00 AM							Family Time
11:30 AM							
12:00 PM	Lunch	Business Networking Lunch	Lunch	Lunch	Lunch		
12:30 PM	Flexible		Flexible	Flexible	Flexible		
1:00 PM							
1:30 PM		Return calls / reply to emails		Research / Prep Presentations			
2:00 PM							
2:30 PM							Open House / Client Appointments
3:00 PM	Client Appointments		Client Appointments		Client Appointments	Personal Time Day Off	
3:30 PM				Business Planning / Tracking & Admin			
4:00 PM		Research / Prep Presentations					
4:30 PM							
5:00 PM							
5:30 PM							
6:00 PM	Family / Dinner Time	Family / Dinner Time	Family / Dinner Time	Family / Dinner Time	Family / Dinner Time		Family / Dinner Time
6:30 PM							
7:00 PM							
7:30 PM							
8:00 PM	Admin Time	Client Appointments	Date Night	Client Appointments	Flexible		Open House Follow-up
8:30 PM							
9:00 PM							

By creating a schedule like the example above you will be able to control your appointments better and run your business like a pro. When a client calls you and says they'd like to see a property, instead of saying "When would you like to go?" you say "Great, I'd love to show you that property. I have time available Monday or Wednesday afternoon or would Tuesday or Thursday evening work better for you?" Now that is a professional way to take control of your schedule and not allow the clients to dictate where you're going and when you need to be there.

Think about it: in what other profession would you simply call the business and demand they see you at a specific time that is convenient for *you*? You don't call the dentist's office and say you want to see the dentist at 2:00 p.m. this afternoon. You don't call the lawyer's office and say you would like to meet with the lawyer in two hours. So, why do we accept that type of behavior in the real estate business? It happens all the time!

Real estate salespeople seem to have become confused about their value proposition. Many feel their availability is what demonstrates their value to the marketplace. I would argue that it is your expertise and not your availability that determines the value you offer your clients. Yes, you must be available when it is necessary, but I don't think it is necessary all the time. Imagine if you called the dentist and every time you called, they answered their phone. Every time you wanted to book an appointment, they were able to accommodate whatever time and day you wanted. You would probably think, "Wow, this person must not be very busy. They answer their phone every time I call them. I can book an appointment any time I want. Maybe they're not very good."

The point I am trying to make here is that, yes, it is important to be responsive to the needs of your clients but be a true professional and take control of your schedule while you are doing that. Offer the clients a couple of options and let them choose from the options you give them.

When it comes to being productive and using your time wisely, it is important to focus on the important things first and not just the urgent ones. Most real estate professionals spend most of their time dealing with the urgent issues which arise daily, and they have no time left to work on the important tasks that will actually grow their business and lead them to higher levels of success. Every day in real estate there are new challenges to overcome and fires to put out. You may have deals falling apart. Frustrated clients. Upset real estate representatives. Conditions that are due. Home inspections that didn't go as well as planned, or maybe a big storm hit, and a tree fell on your car. Any number of things can go sideways. All are seemingly urgent situations you need to deal with right away. The problem is these urgent problems are distractions that take your attention off the important tasks you should be doing every day to build your business.

One of the biggest challenges facing a real estate salesperson is that they need to learn to be disciplined and focus on the not-so-urgent, yet very important activities that are going to lead down the path to success.

This is the major difference between the agent making $35,000 and the agent making $1,000,000. It all comes down to priorities. The low producers run from one fire to the next in a wild frenzy like they are in a full sprint all day long. They say they have no time for any lead-generation activities. They are way too busy for that.

High priority lead generation activities would include things like:

- Connecting with people in your contact sphere
- Coffee meetings or lunches with business partners or past clients
- Attending networking events
- Adding new people to your database

The top producers consistently focus daily on the lead generating tasks that are going to fill their pipeline with good quality leads, and they do it first! They make lead generation their top priority every day, even when they have a million fires burning all around them. I know this probably sounds counterintuitive, but all the pros have mastered it.

Chapter 12

Marketing and Lead Generation

Great marketing requires telling a great story!
—Wayne Throop

When it comes to marketing, there are really two different areas to consider. One is marketing yourself and your business so you can attract new clients. The other is marketing your listings to potential buyers.

Marketing Yourself

To be a great marketer, you have to be a great storyteller. Remember: facts tell, stories sell. Before a client will decide to work with you, they need to know your story. It is more about who you are than it is about what you've done. Sure, you can give them all the information—your stats, how many sales you've done, what awards you've won, blah, blah, blah. But nobody really cares about all that until they like you and trust you to look after their best interests. They really want to get to know you as a person. They're thinking, "Who are you and why would I work with you?" People don't really care how much you know until they know how much you care.

I have found that most people have three basic questions on their minds when it comes to deciding which real estate salesperson they would like to work with:

1. Do I like you?

2. Do I trust you?

3. Do I think you can get the job done?

And those questions are in order of priority for most clients. There is no point talking about how great you are and listing everything you are going to do to help someone buy or sell real estate if they don't already like and trust you. It's important to build rapport with people first. Show interest in them. Be curious. Ask questions. Listen carefully. Find common ground. Get to know them and let them get to know you. Help them understand you are in business to help others, not just to earn a lot of money. Once they like you and trust that your top priority is to serve their best interests you can explain how you are going to help them and why you are the best person for the job.

Who you are becomes your brand. This is the message you consistently communicate when marketing your services. Get the message out there so people know who you are, what you do, and what the benefits are for them when they work with you.

Lead Generation

Generating a steady stream of new leads is probably the single biggest challenge every real estate agent faces. Unfortunately, there is no getting around this one. You must meet this challenge head-on to overcome your fear of rejection and create new opportunities for your business. You must get comfortable with feeling uncomfortable. I believe success in real estate lies just beyond the edge of your comfort zone.

Realistically, most real estate salespeople use only a few different strategies to generate new business and most of your new leads will usually come from a combination of different lead generation techniques that work together.

Typical lead sources include:

1. Referrals from people you know

2. Business networking

3. Open houses

4. Social media marketing

5. Online leads

6. Websites

7. Agent networking

8. Geographic farming

9. Door knocking

10. Cold calling

11. Becoming involved in the community

12. Volunteering

13. Sponsoring events and local sports teams

14. Client parties

15. Office duty

Many of these lead-generation strategies may be uncomfortable at first and you'll possibly get a feeling in the pit of your stomach that says you just don't want to do it. A voice in your head (I call it the "drunk monkey") will be telling you:

"You can't do it."

"This is stupid."

"There must be another way."

"People are going to be annoyed with you for calling them."

"You don't want to bother anyone."

"You don't want to be perceived as that pushy salesperson, do you?"

"You should give up and try something easier."

"This is just a big waste of time."

Don't listen, whatever you do. Find the strategy that best suits your style and keep on going. Push through that discomfort and step outside your comfort zone. Experiment. Try different things. Find what works for you and stick with it. Besides, you have no choice. You have to do it. Your success depends on it.

Marketing Your Listings

Every real estate professional must also become very good at marketing their listings so they can attract the maximum number of potential buyers to come and look at the listing, fall in love with it, and make an offer. This will help you sell the home for the highest possible sale price in the least amount of time, with the least amount of stress and inconvenience for your clients. How are you going to do that? Well, get creative and come up with a great marketing plan and the best way to do that is to start by determining who you feel would be the most likely buyers. What type of home is this and what type of buyer would most likely be interested in it? Is it a small townhome that might appeal to a first-time home buyer or a young family? Is it a larger single-family home that would appeal to a move-up buyer who would like to move to a larger place to raise their family? Could it be someone's dream home? Maybe it's an executive condo downtown that might appeal to younger single professionals? Determining your most likely buyer is always the first step in creating your marketing plan.

Once you've determined the type of buyer you are looking for then you ask yourself where you are going to find them.

A great place to start is online. Will they be on social media? After all, who isn't these days? If so, what platforms would they be using? I would suggest you plan to use the platform your target audience is most likely using daily. My observations indicate the youngest generation of potential homebuyers are currently on Tik Tok and to be perfectly honest, most people in that age group are not in any position financially to purchase a home.

The next cohort would be the people in their mid-twenties-to-late-thirties, and you probably find them using Instagram. The forty-plus crowd is very likely using Facebook and if it is business professionals you are looking for you will most likely find them on LinkedIn. An interesting detail that very few real estate agents seem to be aware of is that users of LinkedIn have the highest average income of any of the social media platforms. If you want to focus your marketing efforts on people who can afford to buy real estate, where do you think you should be focusing your attention?

Social media can be a very effective way to market both your business and your listings. There are plenty of different views about how to use social media effectively for marketing purposes. How frequently should you be posting? Which days of the week are best? Which platforms should you be focusing on? Should you hire a third-party company to manage your social media program? If you were to ask ten experts these questions, you'd probably get ten different sets of opinion. I don't consider myself an expert on social media, but I have learned a few things over the years through my observations of agents who seem to be using it with some success. My advice for most agents who are at least modestly tech savvy, would be to choose one or two social media platforms to focus on, depending on your target audience. Manage it yourself and post at least five times every week on each platform. Not everyone you are connected with is going to see every post you make, so don't be concerned about overdoing it. It's important to remember that it is called "social media" not "business media." The idea is to stay connected and build relationships, not promote your business all the time. Engage in conversations. Like people's posts. Comment on their pictures. Be social.

People will likely find you boring and stop paying attention to your posts if all you do is talk about real estate all the time. If your content is only about your latest new listing, or your next open house, anyone who is not thinking about moving is going to lose interest in your posts very quickly and stop following you.

If social media marketing is going to be part of your business plan, I recommend you dedicate thirty minutes a day to posting messages and connecting with your contacts. Set a timer so you don't get lost in the social media black hole and lose a couple of hours out of your day. I also suggest the best approach is to focus on connecting with people and building relationships first, rather than talking about your real estate business all the time. Sure, it's fine to mention a new listing or an upcoming open house occasionally but remember the true purpose of using social media is to build relationships.

What Should You Say?

Once you know who your target market is and where you are most likely to find them, what are you going to say or do to grab their attention and get them interested in the home you are selling? It all starts with preparation: make the home look its absolute best. Do anything and everything you can to show off the potential the home has to offer. This would include things like improving the curb appeal, making any necessary repairs, decluttering, painting, and cleaning and staging the house. The goal of staging a home is to depersonalize it and organize it in a way that will make it more appealing to the highest number of potential buyers, resulting in a faster sale for more money.

Home staging requires a specialized skill set, a natural aptitude for design and an eye for detail that most real estate agents don't have. As with many things, this job is better left to the professionals, and I recommend hiring a professional home stager to handle this job. Home stagers have a keen sense of interior design, and home decor trends and they understand what will appeal to potential home buyers. Trust me, it will be worth the investment.

Once the house looks perfect, then make it shine online by having a professional photographer take photos and create virtual tours and professional high-quality videos to show the home at its best. Again, this is another aspect of selling a home where I recommend you hire a professional. If you don't believe me, just go online and compare the photos from a listing where the pictures were taken by the agent and a listing where the photos were taken by a professional photographer. You will quickly see a huge difference and understand why professional photography is critical. Remember, 92% of home buyers start their search for a new home online. If they don't like what they see, they won't be booking an appointment to see your listing in person.

There is really no such thing as overdoing it when it comes to preparing a home for sale but be prepared: sometimes you will encounter resistance from the homeowners. Homeowners suddenly become home marketing experts once their house is for sale, and they may try to tell you some of these improvements are not necessary. They are wrong. You are the real estate sales expert. You may need to use some of your expert negotiating skills to convince the seller to do what's necessary to set themselves up for success. At the same time, it's possible the seller just doesn't have time to do the work you feel is necessary or perhaps they must sell quickly. Or maybe they just physically can't do it. Maybe they don't have the budget to pay a contractor to assist them. Maybe they just don't see the value in doing what you are suggesting, and they are hesitant to follow your advice. Whatever the reason, do your best to get them to do as much as possible to prepare their home for the sale.

The next piece of the marketing puzzle is to price it right. Some experts say getting the price right is about 80% of what it takes to sell a home. Pricing a home is never an exact science but this is something you can work on improving. There is often a fine line between pricing it right and overpricing it. Overpricing it by even a small margin might mean the difference between selling quickly or not selling at all. It's tough for many homeowners to wrap their heads around the idea that asking less for their home will likely translate into getting more for it in the long run. In my opinion, there is less risk to underpricing than there is to overpricing it. If you underprice a home, chances are you will attract a lot of interested buyers and very likely receive multiple offers, resulting in a higher sale price. If you overprice it, you will likely see very little interest in your listing and you may end up with a stale listing that just isn't selling.

Here is the ideal outcome: you put the home on the market in perfect condition, price it right, present it online using professional photography and videos, and you attract potential buyers who then book an appointment to view the home in person. They come to see the home and they say: "Wow! This is a nice property, and the price seems very reasonable. I'd better make an offer quickly before someone else does."

On the other hand, if the price is too high, the buyer might not even book an appointment to see the home at all. But if they do, they might be thinking something like: "Nice house but the price seems a little high. Let's wait and see if they decide to lower the price." Or perhaps they say: "Nice home, but why hasn't it sold already? Is there something wrong with it? Why hasn't anyone else bought it?" Neither response is the one you are looking for.

Typically, when you determine the fair market value of a home, you will prepare a Comparative Market Analysis (CMA) for the homeowner. A CMA helps develop an estimate of the fair market value of the home by comparing the listing prices of similar homes currently actively for sale and/or the sale prices of similar homes that have recently sold in the same area. Fair market value simply means the price that represents both the highest price a willing buyer would pay for the home and the lowest price a willing seller would agree to sell it for. Your success in the real estate business will largely depend on your willingness to study the market and become very good at preparing accurate CMAs to ensure the homes you list for sale are priced right and selling in a reasonable time frame.

When it comes to marketing and selling a home, you need to pull out all the stops. Do everything you possibly can to prepare that home, price it right, and professionally present your listing online. If you do all that, then your listings will sell most of the time in any type of market. If you're looking for a good book on marketing, I would recommend you read *Building a Story Brand* by Donald Miller.

Chapter 13

Become An Expert Negotiator

Negotiating isn't all about winning or losing,
it is about finding that perfect place where everyone
walks away feeling good about their decision.
—Wayne Throop

When it comes to negotiation, there is no one-size-fits-all approach that is going to work best 100% of the time. Every negotiation is different. Assess each situation, and the players involved, and determine the best strategy. But make no mistake about it, the ability to negotiate a great deal for your clients is probably one of the most important skills you can develop to add value and become a star in the real estate business. A reputation as a great negotiator will appeal to a broad audience of potential clients. What's more, negotiating is generally something most people don't like to do and it's something they are very willing to pay to have someone else do for them.

You may not consider yourself to be a great negotiator right now but that's okay. Negotiation is a skill you can learn, develop, and become very good at with time and effort. I invite you to study the art of negotiation. Learn from your experiences. Watch how others who are good negotiators handle their negotiations. Read good books and take training courses. Become a student of negotiation. Learn about communication styles and how people like to negotiate. Pay attention to body language and verbal cues when negotiating with others. Each of the parties you're negotiating with has their own unique personality type and negotiating style. The better you understand who you are dealing with the easier things will go during the negotiation.

Effective communication with others is definitely one of the keys to successful negotiations. To become a great negotiator, you would be wise to work on developing something called "emotional intelligence." If you are not already familiar with the concept of emotional intelligence, you should look into it. The term refers to your ability to recognize, control, and express emotions in a way that allows you to relate to others and communicate effectively with them. Having emotional intelligence allows you to recognize and understand the emotional perspective of the people you are communicating with. By developing your emotional intelligence, you will be better able to empathize with the feelings of others and communicate in a way that will resonate with them. Developing your emotional intelligence will inevitably lead to more successful negotiations. If you'd like to learn more about emotional intelligence, I suggest you read a great book by Daniel Goleman called *Emotional Intelligence: Why It Can Matter More Than IQ*.

In addition to developing your emotional intelligence, there are many different personality profiling systems out there which might help you become a better negotiator. I am most familiar with the DISC system. DISC is an acronym for four different personality styles people may have: Dominance (D), Influence (I), Steadiness (S), and Compliance (C). This system provides a framework for quickly identifying the personality traits and communication styles of people you are working with to help you take the right approach and communicate effectively with them in a way they will understand. Everyone can improve at this, with some training.

Here are the characteristics of each communication style:

- **Dominance** describes those individuals with high-drive, get-it-done personalities
- **Influence** describes those who are people oriented, lead with their feelings and appreciate recognition.
- **Steadiness** describes those who are systematic, work at a steady pace, and want what is predictable
- **Compliance** describes people who are detail-oriented and who are often perfectionists. These people feel it's more important to do it right than to get it done fast.

How to communicate with someone who has a strong D personality style:

- Be direct and get to the point quickly (avoid small talk)
- Be on time. They hate having their time wasted
- Focus on the end goal. They are results oriented
- Be specific… "Here is exactly what needs to happen to get your home sold!"

How to communicate with someone who has a strong I personality style:

- Before talking business, take the time to ask how they're doing and what's going on with them
- Engage them in person whenever possible. Don't send them lengthy emails; they won't read them!

Phone calls and video chat messages are the second-best options
- Don't get too detailed or technical (they aren't that interested)
- Bring emotions into what you're saying. "I feel like…"

How to communicate with someone who has a strong S personality style:

- Speak at a steady pace. Create a friendly, relaxed vibe
- Do *not* rush them! Always give them some time to think
- Be prepared to do most of the talking
- Don't be fooled by the "Yes nod"—it doesn't necessarily mean they agree!
- Reassure them. "Take some time and think about what we discussed and get back to me when you're ready."

How to communicate with someone who has a strong C personality style:

- Always come prepared. Do your homework!
- Use logical statements and make sure your facts are correct, and you have details to support your point of view
- Always provide information in writing. They will read detailed emails
- Say something like: "Based on these monthly stats, the facts seem to suggest…"

It is important to keep in mind that most people will have a combination of these styles, but one will typically be more dominant than the others.

The important thing is not so much which personality assessment tool you use as that you become curious about how different styles of communication and different personality types affect the way people like to negotiate. Take time to learn about these different styles. Take time to determine your own preferences. How do you like to communicate? What are your natural tendencies?

Once you understand your own preferences and can assess the personality and communication styles of the people you are working with, you will find the whole negotiation process becomes much easier and less intimidating. You will understand your own personality style and the personality style of the people you are working with, and it will allow you to "speak their language." You will be able to relate to them and communicate in a way that makes sense to them. This means you are far more likely to build rapport, gain trust, and demonstrate your competence, which will inevitably lead to more success in your negotiations and more closed deals for you! Do yourself a favor and learn as much as you can about emotional intelligence and communication and personality styles... and become an expert at the art of negotiation. You might even find you start to enjoy it!

If you would like more information on the DISC personality profiling system, I would recommend you connect with Victoria Theriault who has a company called "DISCover What Works." Victoria is a certified facilitator of DISC and EQ and uses these platforms for individual and team coaching. She also hosts an excellent podcast that examines how to communicate optimally with others.

Fortunately, in the real estate business, most of the negotiating we do is not a matter of life or death, but it *is* a pretty big deal for most people. In most cases, we are dealing with the single biggest financial asset most people will ever own. It can be very important for them in the future to make sure they maximize the return on their investment. Here are a few strategies to help you get started towards becoming a better negotiator.

Set Yourself Up for Success: My Top Five Tips to Become a Better Negotiator

1. Do Your Homework
   a. Know all the facts about the situation (knowledge is power).
   b. Know who the key players are (understand their communication style).

2. Focus on Relationships First
   a. Build rapport with the other players involved.
   b. Listen carefully to understand their priorities.
   c. Search for win-win opportunities.

3. Keep Your Emotions in Check
   a. Stay calm under pressure (a calm state of mind leads to better decisions).
   b. Avoid being confrontational.

4. Find Common Ground
   a. Be prepared to compromise: you can't always get everything you want in a negotiation. Look for areas you can easily agree on.

THE REALITY OF REAL ESTATE

b. Ask for something you don't really want and be prepared to give it up.
c. Consider items included in a deal or terms and conditions other than money that might be agreeable to all parties.

5. Know when to walk away.
a. Understand that line in the sand, where it will no longer make sense for your clients to proceed.
b. Be prepared to walk away and pursue other opportunities.

To learn more about effective negotiation techniques and strategies, I recommend you read a book called *Never Split the Difference: Negotiating as If Your Life Depended on It* written by Chris Voss, a former hostage negotiator for the FBI. This book talks about some of the negotiation tactics he used while he was with the FBI and explains how some of these same strategies can be applied in everyday life (including real estate deals).

Chapter 14

Become a World Class Communicator

It is not so much what you say.
It is more about how you make people
feel that they will remember.
—Wayne Throop

I think that if all real estate salespeople were more aware of this basic principle, they'd be a lot more successful: We have two ears and one mouth. Listen twice as much as you speak! Most salespeople seem to do most of the talking and none of the listening. Communication is not just all about talking. The great agents seem to have this figured out. Most of them are great listeners.

So, what exactly makes a great listener? I would say a great listener is genuinely interested in hearing what another person has to say without trying to formulate their response while the other person is still talking. They are attentive and eager to understand the other person. They are dialed in, and present in the moment. You can think of listening as a muscle. The more you exercise that muscle, the stronger it becomes and the better you get at it.

One technique you can use to improve your listening skills is called "mirroring." Basically, you ask a question, listen carefully to the other person's response then repeat back to them exactly what they just said, word for word, and ask if that was what they meant to say. Be curious, pause, and listen again to the response. Sometimes, they might say, "no, that is not what I meant," and they'll rephrase what they were saying. You can repeat this process until you are 100% clear on what they are trying to say.

Another key to effective communication and becoming a great listener is to be curious and show the other person you care about them. Ask great questions and pause. Allow the other person time to formulate their response. Give them the opportunity to express their thoughts and ideas before you start talking again. After they finish talking, pause and then repeat what they've said to make sure you heard them correctly. Show this person you are genuinely listening and are interested in what they are saying. Show them you care. Remember: people don't care how much you know until they know how much you care.

Here is a story I can share with you that will illustrate how *not* to communicate. Years ago, when I was selling real estate, I recognized the importance of having a good network of solid business relationships and I had a close inner circle of like-minded self-employed business professionals whom I could recommend to my clients. These were trusted partners, and I knew I could count on them to provide excellent service and take great care of my clients. I was also always trying to add new professionals to my network so we could build mutually beneficial business relationships. I was very particular about my recommendations: they had to be top professionals in their field. If I was working with a client who needed help obtaining financing, I had people I could refer them to. Or if people needed help with virtually anything from painters to plumbers, lawyers, accountants, home inspectors, and even carpet cleaners, you name it, I had a reliable connection I could refer them to. And in return, these same business professionals would do the same for me. If they met someone looking for some help either buying or selling a home, they would refer those people to me.

At one stage of my career, I was referred to a new client who happened to be a mortgage advisor for one of the lenders in town. I helped her buy a home and we started to build a connection; a business relationship was starting to blossom. In time, she started to refer some of her clients to me. In fact, I actually sold six homes to clients she had referred to me in one year. And even more importantly, these were not cheap homes. The cheapest of the homes I sold was $350,000 and that was in 2006. Imagine what that would be in today's dollars! Needless to say, it was a very lucrative source of income for me.

As time went on, I knew I needed to reciprocate. Any successful business relationship needs to be a two-way street. It can't be all one sided. So, I started referring some of my clients to this person. The first couple of times it didn't work out and I didn't really ask my clients why. They just went on and found someone else to help them. But after four or five attempts to refer my clients to the same mortgage advisor, I started to get curious. Why did they not want to work with this person? What exactly was the problem? At first, my clients wouldn't really say why, they would just say she wasn't a good fit for them and asked if I could refer them to someone else. Finally, after a couple of more referrals that didn't work out, I got my answer.

One client who I had referred to this mortgage advisor was very willing to share her thoughts on why she didn't want to work with this person. She said, "we met with her for about forty-five minutes, and she really didn't listen to us or hear anything we wanted to say. She just talked about herself for the entire time. How great she was. How busy she was. How many deals she was doing every year. What sales awards she was receiving. The fancy car she was driving. The posh resort she was going to for her vacation. How many rounds of golf she had played that summer. We could barely get a word in edgewise. We certainly didn't get the impression she cared about us or what our concerns were, or what we needed help with. We want to work with someone who cares about what is important to us."

What's In It for Them?

Wow! That was great feedback and also a great reminder for me, in my own business. I think this is a common problem real estate representatives need to be aware of. When it comes to effective communication, the conversation is not all about you. What people are most interested in is what's in it for them. Do you care about them? How are you going to deliver value and how is it going to benefit them? They don't want to hear about how great you think you are or how many deals you've done or even what awards you've won. I hate to break it to you, but nobody really cares (other than maybe a few other real estate salespeople). People want to talk about what is important to *them* and they want to feel heard.

Effective communication is all about listening carefully and showing people you care. Eliminate the distractions. Put your phone away. Be present. Give people your full attention. I've heard it said that attention is the new currency. Everyone is craving attention. As one of my real estate colleagues, Hanna Browne, once said, "Wherever you are, be there!"

Attracting your attention is a big deal and big companies are spending big money fighting for it through various forms of marketing and advertising. Smartphones are high on that list. They can be a great asset, but they can also be a major distraction. If you can find a way to become a world class listener and eliminate distractions from your communications with others, you are going to set yourself apart from most of your competitors. People want to feel like they have been heard, that you care about them, and that you are present and genuinely interested in what they are saying. So, if you want to become a more effective communicator, listen more than you speak and pay attention to what the other person is saying. Show them you care. Be present in that moment.

If you are looking to improve your communication skills, you might consider joining a public speaking organization like Toastmasters. When most people think of Toastmasters, they probably think of public speaking, and I did too, but I quickly found out it is as much about listening as it is about speaking. I was part of a Toastmasters group for about three years, and I would highly recommend it for all real estate representatives—or anyone else who plans to set themselves apart from the competition and become a true professional at the top of their industry. During a Toastmasters meeting, members will take on various roles. Some are speaking roles; others are active listening roles. Either way, if you are participating consistently in these meetings and taking on different roles each week, you are going to notice a dramatic improvement in your overall communication, but especially your listening skills.

As we've been seeing throughout this chapter, you need to master two important aspects of effective communication if you plan to enjoy a high level of success in the real estate business. One is how you speak, i.e., what you say and how you deliver your message. But if you ask me, the more important piece—Part Two of effective communication—is your ability to listen attentively and actually hear what people are trying to say. Master those two concepts and you're on the fast track to success in the real estate world.

Chapter 15

Creating and Managing Systems

*Success requires consistency and consistency
is achieved through creating systems.*
—Wayne Throop

The real estate business can get very chaotic at times and as your business grows and you start working with increasing numbers of clients, it will become increasingly important to use your time wisely. The best way to use your time efficiently and stay organized is to create systems for those things you do repeatedly. A system is just a series of documented steps (e.g., a checklist) of the steps you are going to take every time you perform a specific task. You can have a system for almost anything you do on a regular basis.

That might include things like:

1. Lead generation/business development.

2. Lead follow-up and conversion.

3. Managing client data (using a CRM).

4. Tracking business activities.

5. Business planning.

6. Expense tracking and budgeting.

7. Running an open house.

8. Preparing Comparative Market Analyses (CMA).

9. Booking listing appointments.

10. Managing the listing process.

11. Working with buyers from contract to closing.

12. The transaction process.

13. Offer preparation, planning, and completion.

14. A client appreciation program.

15. A client for life/stay in touch program.

16. Posting on social media.

There are likely other systems you could come up with, as well, but this list is a good starting point.

Systems have many advantages. First of all, they take the guesswork out of the common tasks you perform daily. You follow specific steps every time you do something. Systems ensure consistency in the delivery of your services, and they lead to predictable results.

You might be thinking you are not busy enough to worry about having systems in place at this point in your career. Well, I've found that the best time to create and implement systems is *before* you get busy, not after. Once you start getting busy, you are undoubtedly going to feel overwhelmed, and you won't have the time you need to create and put systems in place. It is far better to be proactive than reactive. Do yourself a favor and create these systems before you feel like you need them.

To illustrate the benefits of a good system, I'd like to share how I benefited from creating an "Open House" system. Over time, I came up with a very specific series of steps I followed for every open house I did. I must admit it wasn't perfect the first time I tried it. Coming up with a great system involves some trial and error. You try something and if it doesn't work then you tweak it and try again until you land on the winning formula. But here is the system I came up with to produce a very successful open house virtually every time I did one:

1. Decide on the location, date, and time for the Open House at least one week in advance (in many areas these are typically held on a Sunday afternoon from 2:00 p.m. to 4:00 p.m.).

2. Install Open House sign toppers advertising the date and time for the open house seven days ahead. If the open house is on a Sunday, then the sign goes up by the Monday before, at the latest.

3. On Wednesday, touch base with my clients to give them a checklist of everything I need them to do prior to their Open House.

Sample Seller's Open House Preparation Checklist

The following checklist was created to take the guesswork out of what a seller needs to do to prepare their home for an open house.

Interior:

- ❑ Ensure your home is spotless
- ❑ Empty cat litter boxes
- ❑ Vacuum and/or wash floors
- ❑ Clean windows as needed
- ❑ Dust surfaces
- ❑ Clean appliances
- ❑ Wipe counters in kitchen and bathrooms
- ❑ Put away all dishes
- ❑ Empty laundry baskets
- ❑ Put away clean laundry
- ❑ Make all beds
- ❑ Ensure bedrooms are tidy
- ❑ Empty all garbage cans and recycling bins inside the home
- ❑ Neatly store kids' toys
- ❑ Put away dog beds and toys
- ❑ Ensure the home has a pleasant smell but do not overdo it with air fresheners
- ❑ Ensure the home is a comfortable temperature
- ❑ Open windows to allow fresh air in when appropriate
- ❑ Put all valuables away in a safe location

Exterior:

One of the keys to a successful open house is creating a great first impression for potential buyers as they arrive at your home. A well-maintained home with a nicely landscaped yard can go a long way towards successfully selling your home at a great price. Curb appeal is critical!

- ❑ Tidy garage/put loose items in Rubbermaid bins to store neatly
- ❑ Put kids' toys, bikes and other sports equipment away
- ❑ Cut grass
- ❑ Tidy gardens, trim shrubs, pull weeds as needed
- ❑ During dry periods, water grass, flower beds, and shrubs to ensure a healthy green appearance
- ❑ In the winter remove snow and ice from the driveway and sidewalks to ensure safe access
- ❑ Ensure eavestroughs are cleaned out and downspouts are installed properly
- ❑ Neatly arrange furniture on your deck, patio, or balcony
- ❑ Repair obvious deficiencies and imperfections on the exterior of your home or property

4. On Thursday, call people in your database who may be interested in a home like the one where you are hosting the Open House, or who may have family or friends who might be interested. (Invite at least ten people).

5. Call and invite people you've met at recent open houses for similar properties.

6. On Friday, hand out invitations to neighbors near the property where you are hosting the Open House to let them know about it and invite them to join you. Ask them to also invite any family members or friends who may be interested in moving into the neighborhood. (Knock on doors at ten homes on either side of the listing and ten homes across the street).

7. Print full-color feature sheets and prepare any other marketing materials you plan to bring to the Open House.

8. On Saturday, drive by the property where you are hosting your Open House to make sure the property looks its best and call the sellers to remind them about completing all the tasks on the checklist you provided.

9. Conduct research on the MLS system to review the most recent sales and active listings in the area. Print out a list of all houses in the area that have sold over the past six months as well as all homes currently for sale.

10. On Sunday morning before 9:00 a.m. put out as many "Open House" directional signs as possible on every corner of the neighborhood so people can find your Open House. (I used between eight and twelve directional signs, depending on the neighborhood). Leave those signs out as long as possible to maximize your exposure in that community.

11. Pick up snacks, refreshments, and a bouquet of flowers for your Open House. I would recommend you keep it simple and bring snacks that are easy to eat and not too messy (I typically went with Lindt chocolates). I typically left the flowers in the home for the sellers to enjoy after the Open House.

12. On Sunday afternoon, arrive in the neighborhood where your Open House is being held at least thirty minutes before it starts. Drive around the immediate

area to refresh your memory and look for any new developments that may be coming soon.

13. Arrive at your Open House twenty minutes before the scheduled start time. Your clients should be gone by now. Check to make sure everything looks good. The home should be neat and tidy. Valuables must have been put away. Lights should be on, and all curtains left open. Make sure some soft background music is playing and the temperature in the home is comfortable. The goal is to create a welcoming environment that is going to encourage potential buyers to take their time and stay longer.

14. Prior to people's arrival, neatly put out your snacks and refreshments, your guest registry, and your marketing materials.

15. Host a professional open house. Don't be too pushy. Engage in conversation with potential buyers. Build rapport. Give them some space. Find a reason to follow-up. Be sure to get contact information from your guests. Bonus tip: rather than giving out business cards to potential buyers, take a picture of your business card on your phone and offer to text it to people. Now you have their cell phone number.

16. After the Open House, return the home to the state it was in when you arrived. Lock doors, turn out all lights, and turn off the music.

17. Write a thank you note to the sellers with a summary of how things went and leave it on the kitchen table

with the flowers. Mention you will follow-up with a phone call later.

18. On Sunday evening send a follow-up email to every guest for whom you have an email address. Thank them for coming. Ask if they have any feedback about the property and if they have any questions you can answer for them.

19. Before it gets dark, pick up all your "Open House" directional signs.

20. Call to give the sellers an update on how things went and what you are going to be doing to follow-up with potential buyers.

21. Send a handwritten thank you note to any potential buyers for whom you have a mailing address. Remember, in many cases this information can be looked up online.

22. On Monday, follow up by phone with any potential buyers who may be interested or who have questions. (Don't give up if you aren't able to connect with them the first time you try. Keep trying!)

So, this is an example of what a good system might look like. By following these steps consistently, I knew I would be able to host a very productive and successful open house most of the time.

I recall going into my office on Monday mornings and hearing other agents griping and complaining about how nobody had come to their open houses the previous day, meanwhile I had just had at least twenty people come to mine. The big difference was that I had been following a system and they hadn't. I suggest that if you are going to take your valuable time to host an open house on a weekend, why not make the best of it? Create a system you can follow to produce consistent and predictable results.

This is just one example, but if you want to be as organized and productive as you can possibly be, you will need to create systems for every task you perform on a regular basis. Make no mistake about it, having systems is one of the keys to success in the real estate business.

Oh, and one piece of advice about open houses: don't plan any other appointments just before or right after an open house. It's just too stressful. When I was selling real estate, I had a policy that I would never book appointments with any clients before my open houses but there was one time when I compromised on that policy, and I learned a valuable lesson the hard way. I was hosting an open house on a Sunday afternoon from 2:00 p.m. to 4:00 p.m. Normally, I liked to arrive about thirty minutes early to make sure the house was in perfect showing condition and to prepare myself for the potential buyers who would come to view the property. I hate a last-minute scramble for anything I do, but especially open houses. This time, though, I had a client who absolutely insisted I take him to view a property he had his eye on and, of course, he just had to go Sunday afternoon. I realized he wasn't going to back down on this so, to keep my client happy, I grudgingly agreed to show it to him. But I was very clear I had to be wrapped up by 1:00 p.m. at the latest to ensure I had enough time to drive from that house over to my Open House.

I looked it up online and determined that it would take about twenty-five minutes to drive from one house to the other. *No problem*, I thought to myself. *I can pull this off and still make it to my Open House in plenty of time.* Well, guess what? Buddy shows up forty-five minutes late for the showing appointment. It is now 12:45 p.m. I had booked our showing from 12:00 p.m. to 1:00 p.m. *No problem,* I thought to myself, *we still need to be out by 1:00 p.m. so he'll just have to be quick, right?* Not so much. He proceeded to take a full forty-five minutes to view this home. It's now 1:30 p.m. and I have a twenty-five-minute drive to get to my Open House.

I am very stressed at this point. I fly across town and at 1:55 p.m. I pull into the driveway where my Open House is being held. Of course, there are people who have arrived early, waiting at the door wondering where I am. (Not very professional on my part.) I reach into the trunk in a fluster to grab what I needed. Somehow, I managed to slice a big gash in the top of my hand on the sharp corner of one of my "Open House" directional signs. Blood everywhere! Now what? There I am, no first aid kit, no bandages, not even any sort of clean cloth or paper towel, nothing. And I am bleeding all over the place.

I quickly slap my opposite hand on top of the cut to apply pressure to slow down the bleeding. I make my way to the front door, introduce myself (no shaking of hands this time) and find a way to open the lock box, get the key out and unlock the door. By this point there is a decent-sized pool of blood on the front step of that house. Both my hands are covered in blood, and I have blood stains on my pants. What a mess.

The buyers must have thought I was some kind of crazy person. "Are you okay?" they asked. "I'll be fine. It's just a little scratch. Nothing too serious." But in my mind, I'm thinking *okay, now what?* Here I am at the front door of my clients' house, blood dripping from my hand all over everything, and I have nothing to put on it to stop the bleeding.

Luckily my client's home had a powder room just inside the front door and as fate would have it, I was able to find a roll of paper towels under the sink. I grabbed a few sheets of paper towel and was able to get the bleeding under control fairly quickly. Fortunately, I managed to sop up the pools of blood which had dripped on the floor and most of the front step before any other guests arrived, but what a stressful (and embarrassing) situation I had put myself in!

The moral of this story actually has two parts. First, you should always have a first aid kit in your car, just in case of an emergency like this one and, more importantly, *never* book another appointment just before an open house. It is just not worth it!

Chapter 16

Tracking Your Business Daily

If you track your business activities and results,
you will always know exactly where you stand
and can make adjustments as needed.
—Wayne Throop

There is one area of the real estate business that is often overlooked and poorly managed by most agents. That is the tracking of their daily activities, their new leads, and their ongoing business results. Most agents have no formal system for tracking any of these areas and those who do tend to be very inconsistent with their implementation. The problem is that without a proper system in place you have no way of knowing what you need to do to produce the results you are looking for. Without tracking systems your business is very unpredictable. If you want a business that runs like a business, you need tracking systems.

So, what exactly should you be tracking? One area you should track is everything you are doing proactively to generate new business. How many phone calls are you making to your contacts and business partners every day? How many lunch or coffee meetings are you attending? How many personal handwritten notes are you sending? How many clients have you stopped by to visit? How many social media posts are you making every day? How many texts or emails are you sending? What about videos? How many of those are you sending every day? Seriously, it's important you know exactly what actions you are taking proactively every day to generate new business and how many of them result in a new lead.

Once you determine what you must do to generate a new lead, then track how many new leads generate one sale. This will tell you precisely how many leads you need in order to generate the number of sales that will allow you to achieve your income goals. Is it five leads per sale? Ten Leads? The other thing you must consider is that these numbers are likely to fluctuate throughout the year as the market changes. There may be times when you must do more to produce fewer new leads, and there will likely be other times when you are able to do less and generate more new leads. It is relative to what is going on in the real estate market at the time.

So, what exactly would a tracking system look like? The good news is, there is no need to reinvent the wheel. There are many systems already available. Many CRM systems have very slick tracking capabilities that even people who are not extremely tech savvy find easy to use. If you are even the slightest bit comfortable with using technology, you'll find these systems very straight- forward and easy to implement.

If you are not exactly comfortable with technology you might try an old-school, paper-based system very similar to one I used many years ago when I sold real estate. (Refer to the sample tracking sheet on the next page.) Simply print off a new page every month and put it in a binder. As you complete a lead-generating activity you simply circle the number that represents how many of that type of activity you have now completed that month. The nice thing about a system like this is that it can be very motivating. Every time I'd start a new month, my immediate goal would be to surpass the number of lead-generating activities I had completed the previous month. Eventually, I started to notice that the fuller these pages were at the end of the month, the more business I was doing. The activities you are keeping track of are only the proactive things you are doing to attract new business and/or build relationships. How easy is that?

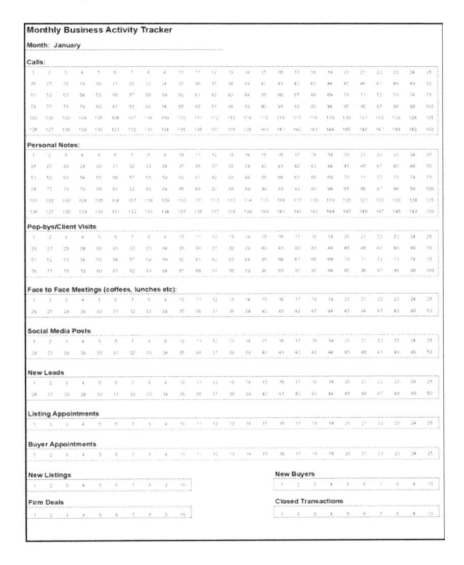

It can be a challenge to figure out when and how to record these activities. Here is an example of what often happens to a real estate salesperson: You are out at a social gathering, maybe a holiday or birthday party, and someone asks you what you do for a living. You tell them you are in real estate and that you help people buy and sell homes. They ask how the market is and mention they are thinking about moving in the next six-to-eight months. They invite you to call them in a few months to follow up because they might be interested in your help. Throughout the remainder of the evening, you have two more similar conversations with people who are also considering moving within the next year or so. You're out the next night at a different function and the same thing happens. What are you going to do with all that information? How are you going to keep track of it, so you don't forget to follow up?

Did you get their contact information?

You can offer to text them your contact information, which enables you to obtain their cell phone number. You should also need to make some notes at the earliest possible opportunity, even if these are just brief bullet points on a piece of paper or a voice memo on your cell phone. After you get home and have an opportunity to jump on a computer, you should immediately enter whatever contact information you have, plus a few basic notes, into your CRM. You should also set a reminder for yourself to follow up with those people at the appropriate time. Ideally, you will do this as soon as possible—if not the same night, then do it first thing the next morning while everything is still fresh in your mind. If you are using a paper-based activity or lead tracking system, don't forget to update that as well.

My recommendation is to also send each of these people a personal note letting them know you would be happy to assist them when they are ready; provide your business card with your contact information. When it comes to following up with any new leads you've developed, don't forget you should always cut the timeframe they gave you in half, and make sure you reach out to them at that point. When people start talking about moving, they often accelerate the process and things move much faster than they had originally anticipated. Six months can become three months very quickly. If you wait too long, you might just find you missed out on the opportunity.

All the new leads you come up with should be added to your pipeline of future opportunities. This is another system you should have, whether it is built into your CRM or a spreadsheet (if you have an old-fashioned paper-based system). You could even use a whiteboard in your office, if you're not concerned about your colleagues seeing what you have going on.

Within your system you should always categorize each lead based on when you anticipate they will buy or sell, and how serious they are. It is good to have a variety of leads with some likely to come to fruition in the short term, some likely to happen in the medium term and some being longer-term opportunities.

Regardless of how you decide to categorize your leads, the most important thing is that you have some form of system in place to keep track of who your leads are and where they are in the process. You can also assign an approximate dollar amount for each lead so you can forecast your future earnings potential based on the leads you currently have.

Capture the Relevant Information

Once your leads turn into actual business, and you help someone buy or sell a property, you need another system to keep track of your closed transactions. Again, this could be done within a CRM if the one you are using has that capability, or you can use a spreadsheet to capture all the relevant information. You should keep track of the address of the property, the clients' names, the list price, the sale price, the closing date, and the amount of commission you received. As time goes on and you track this information year after year, you will find it makes life a lot easier when it comes to forecasting future business and preparing your annual business plan. It may also prove to be very valuable should you decide to retire and sell your business to another agent.

Although there are probably countless other systems you could come up with to help you track and manage your business, the last one I am going to talk about is a system for tracking your business expenses. You should always know how much you are spending so you can regularly compare the amount to your income. I suggest you use some form of accounting software, or even a basic spreadsheet, to keep track of your expenses and then prepare a profit-and-loss statement monthly or, at a bare minimum, at least quarterly. Many agents don't exactly enjoy doing this, and many are not very good at it, for that matter, so you may need some help from either a bookkeeper or an accountant, or possibly both. The important thing is not how it gets done, it is that you are doing it consistently and reviewing your profitability regularly.

Imagine how you would feel if you were considering investing in a business whose owners had no idea how profitable they were and they couldn't tell you? Probably not very good! As a business owner, you should always know where you stand financially. You should also be assessing where you are spending money and determining if you are getting a good return on those investments. Are they worth it? If you are not tracking your expenses, you won't know. By creating a system to keep track of your business expenses, you'll very quickly be able to recognize whether an investment is bringing you a good rate of return or whether you should consider investing in something else. Why waste your hard-earned money on things that are not working? Things like the bus bench that is costing you $250 per month, or the ad on the bulletin board at the grocery store that costs you $1,000 for the year, or the $800 to be on the placemat at the local family restaurant. You should always be asking every new client how they heard of you. How did they find you? The better you understand what's working and what isn't, and where you are with your expenses on an on-going basis, the better position you will be in to make wise decisions regarding your spending.

Chapter 17

Creating and Managing Systems Around Relationships

One of the most important things every
successful businessperson should know is that
people do business with people they like!
—Wayne Throop

One of the nice things about the real estate business is that if you want to be successful you only have to look at what the successful agents are doing and copy them. Success leaves clues, just copy what is already working for others.

If you ask most experienced, successful real estate representatives. I am confident they would say most of their business comes from either repeat clients or referrals from people they already know. Not from cold calling. Not from chasing random internet leads. Not from expensive print advertising. All they do is follow a system to stay in touch with their past clients and other people they know. And repeat and referral clients almost always tend to be the best people to work with. They will follow your advice, appreciate everything you do for them, and most of the time, they won't even ask you for a discount on your fee. Cold leads, on the other hand, are often difficult to work with. They don't mind wasting your time. They rarely follow your advice. They are a pain to work with from start to finish. They never appreciate what you do for them, and they almost always insist that if you don't give them a discount, they won't work with you. Who would you prefer to focus your time and attention on?

You might be thinking, *why would I need a system to stay in touch with the people I already know? I am already doing that without a system.* You may also be thinking this seems artificial or insincere. You feel like the only reason you are staying in touch is because you want something from the people to whom you are connected. The truth is, yes, you do want something... but that is not the primary reason why you are staying connected. You are staying connected because you genuinely care about these people. You are making sure they have access to the best qualified real estate professional if and when they—or one of their friends—need help buying or selling a property, which just happens to be the most expensive investment most people will ever make. You are making sure they consider you to be their trusted advisor whenever the subject of real estate comes up.

When you are starting out in the real estate business you may feel a formal system for staying connected with the people you already know is not necessary because you don't have very many connections. You may feel you can manage this on your own by randomly doing whatever you want, whenever you want, to reach out to those people, just as you always did prior to your career in real estate. Well, that may be true for a short period of time but as your business grows and you become more successful and work with more clients, it becomes increasingly difficult to manage without a proper system to follow. And the best time to create a system is before you need it. Once you get too busy, you won't have time to implement the system properly and you'll be running around like a crazy person and very likely missing out on working with a lot of great clients.

A number of referral-based systems are available, but most have a few common elements. My recommendation would be to investigate a few different options and see which one resonates most with you. Consider going out for lunch or coffee with a more experienced agent who has had some success building a referral-based business and pick their brain. Ask them which system they are using and what they like about it. Ask them which one they would recommend you adopt.

Most of the systems I am familiar with involve touching all your connections two or three times a month, or about twenty-four-to-thirty-six touches per year. I know you're probably thinking that sounds like a lot, and you're afraid your people will get annoyed with you and perceive you as a "pushy salesperson." That is a very common excuse I hear all the time from people who aren't staying in touch with their connections consistently enough to build a successful referral-based business. The truth is, there is a lot of noise out there and it is extremely difficult to grab people's attention. Just because you are reaching out two or three times a month doesn't mean people are noticing every single contact.

The key to avoid annoying people or being perceived as a pushy salesperson is to provide value. Every time you reach out to a contact make sure you are providing them with information that might be valuable to them. Perhaps it is information about a recent sale in their neighborhood. Maybe it is information around a new listing that just came up on their street. Maybe it is the latest update on housing prices in the area. Or the number of sales in their neighborhood over the past twelve months. Maybe it is information on new government housing incentives or programs. An update on the latest interest rates. A forecast for the housing market for the next year. You are not asking them for business every time you talk to them (that would get annoying very quickly). You are providing them with useful information they might find helpful. You want them to think of you as their very own real estate resource center, a trusted advisor they can count on whenever they need help with something related to real estate.

So, what are the things you should be doing to stay connected with your contacts on a regular basis? Well, I would suggest you should have a phone conversation with most of your key supporters at least once a quarter. For your biggest advocates, I would recommend once a month, at least. In between those phone calls, you should probably plan at least a couple of coffee meetings and perhaps a lunch meeting once or twice a year.

Send a Monthly Newsletter!

You should also be sending out some valuable information through a newsletter to all your contacts every month as well. You should also be connecting with people through your social media channels by liking and commenting on their posts regularly. Again, you're not always banging the drums about real estate in every conversation. You're just connecting with your key people like any normal person would do. And whenever you do ask for their help, you should always keep it subtle. If they ask you how the real estate market is doing, you might say, "it's great but we are low on inventory of homes for sale right now. Who do you know who might be thinking of moving?"

That's it, that's all. You'll notice this is not a "yes" or "no" question. They have to think about this and when they do, you might just get a referral.

Hosting a client party for your key supporters a couple of times a year is another great way to stay connected. Think about it. Hosting a party gives you multiple opportunities to connect with your people. First, you send them an email or text message telling them about your event and asking them to save the date. Then you send out the invitation asking them to RSVP if they are planning to attend. If you don't hear back from them, then you should follow-up with a phone call to make sure they received your invitation. Ask if they are going to be able to join you. A day or two before your event you should call everyone to remind them about the time and location of your party. Then you host a great party. Perhaps you even tie it in with some form of fundraiser for a local charity or the foodbank. Take a few pictures of you with your clients having a great time. Post the pictures on your social media platforms and then send a handwritten thank you note with a picture of the person and their family at your party having a blast. What a great opportunity to stay connected and build relationships!

There are a few other things you can do to stay connected and top of mind with your key people. For example, birthday or holiday cards. You can do video messages such as "Happy New Year" or "Happy Holidays" messages. It doesn't matter so much what you are doing, exactly, but it is very important you have some structure around what you are doing and that you are following a system to ensure consistency. Remember, it is not what you are doing occasionally that will determine your success, it is all about what you are doing consistently that matters.

Doing the right things consistently will lead you to tremendous success in the long term. Remember that a career in real estate is like a marathon, not a sprint. There is no quick road to success. You don't just flick a switch and suddenly find you're a successful real estate agent. Success requires consistent action following a systematized approach over an extended period and a lot of patience and persistence.

If you are looking for information on systems that will help you stay in touch with people you already know, I would recommend you check out the following lead generation systems:

- Buffini & Company: Work by Referral System
- Richard Robbins International: Lifetime Referral System
- KiTS Keep in Touch Systems Program

Chapter 18

Integrity and Professionalism

Having integrity and conducting yourself like a true professional
should be considered mandatory for all real estate agents
—Wayne Throop

I have to be honest with this one. The lack of professionalism in the real estate industry has long been a sore point for me. It's not surprising to me that the public generally has a very low opinion of real estate salespeople. The bar is very low at times in this industry. Unethical behavior is far too common. Greed sets in. The real estate salesperson starts to act in their own best interest and not the best interest of their clients. These things happen, people talk about it, and the word about our industry spreads. People's trust in real estate agents diminishes. It's unfortunate, but they start to think all real estate representatives are like that. Thankfully, I can assure you that is not the case.

The good news is that there is an easy solution to this problem. We must weed out those bad apples from the industry and ensure those who remain just follow the Golden Rule and treat others the way we'd like to be treated.

Here is an example of what I mean. Some variation of this type of unethical behavior happens from time to time, and I cringe every time I hear something like this. The story begins with a less-than-ethical real estate salesperson who somehow convinces a seller they should list their home with them. They probably offered a substantial discount on their commission fee just to get the listing and the seller, who is looking to save a few bucks, falls for it. Remember the old saying: "you get what you pay for." Another gem is, "If you pay peanuts then you get monkeys." The homeowner has unknowingly just hired an unethical salesperson who is focused solely on their own paycheck and who cares very little about the seller's best interest or the ultimate selling price of the home. But that seller thinks they're going to save money. Really? Think about it. If someone can't negotiate their own paycheck, how can you possibly expect them to negotiate the best deal on your home?

The agent does the bare minimum to prepare and market the home, but they price it low and hope for the best. Somehow, they manage to encourage a couple of buyers to call to see the place. (Even a blind squirrel finds a nut once in a while). The agent shows the house to the buyers, but they are not ready to make an offer just yet. They want to think about it. The listing agent is salivating with visions of sugar plums dancing in their head just imagining what they are going to do with that big fat commission check if they can double-end the deal.

They tell the buyers they have had a lot of interest in the property, and they had better not wait too long before making an offer. Meanwhile only two buyers have seen the property at this point and there have been no other inquiries. The next day, another agent representing a buyer shows the listing to their client. They like the house and would like to make an offer. The listing agent says they will need at least twenty-four hours to consider any offers because his clients are "out of town" and won't be able to consider the offer until the next day around 7:00 p.m. "Don't worry, though," he says, "we are not anticipating any other offers at this point."

The honest and ethical buyer's agent takes what the listing agent says at face value and submits their offer at 7:00 p.m. They reluctantly give the full twenty-four hours to the sellers so they can have enough time to consider the offer. The asking price for the home was $859,000 and the buyers have submitted an initial offer at $845,000 with only one condition for a home inspection because they really want to buy this home, and they would like to get a deal put together before someone else decides to submit an offer.

The buyer's agent submits the offer to the listing agent and the buyers anxiously await a response from the sellers. As soon as the listing agent receives the offer, they immediately contact both of the buyers they had shown the property to and tell them they have received an offer on the property, and they had better step up and prepare an offer as well, if they are interested. They put the hard sell on these two buyers and suggest they could get a better deal by purchasing through the listing agent because they can offer the seller a discount on their commission. It turns out that one of the two buyers is considering making an offer, but they must check with the bank regarding their financing, so they won't be able to do anything until the next day. The listing agent says, "no problem, we don't need to respond to the first offer for twenty-four hours."

The listing agent calls the seller and tells them about the offer they received but mentions they are working on one of their own offers for a client they showed the property to so they should wait on responding to the first offer. "No rush, we have twenty-four hours to respond." In the meantime, the listing agent drags their feet in responding to the buyer's agent and fails to fill them in on what is going on in a timely fashion.

At this point, the first buyers have no clue about what's happening on the sellers' side. As far as they know the sellers are "out of town" and hard to reach. By 3:00 p.m. on the second day (twenty hours from when they first submitted their offer), the buyer's agent still hasn't heard anything from the listing agent despite several attempts to reach them by every means possible (phone calls, texts, and emails). The buyers are extremely nervous and anxious to hear any news from the sellers. Boy, that listing agent sure must be busy considering they probably only have that one listing.

What has really been happening is that the listing agent has been dragging their feet responding to the buyer's agent while they have been pestering the other potential buyers they showed the property to, begging them to submit some form of offer so they can create a competing offer situation. So far, that first buyer's agent has not been told there is any other interest in the property. Finally, around 4:00 p.m., with about three hours to spare before the first offer expires, the second buyer reluctantly decides to proceed with an offer. They have decided to offer $825,000 with no conditions. The listing agent recommends they only give the seller four hours to make a decision.

Finally, the listing agent contacts the first buyer's agent and says "sorry about the delay getting back to you, my clients have been very difficult to reach. You won't believe this, but out of nowhere, I just had a buyer call me directly and ask me to prepare an offer on the property for them. Wow! What a surprise! We now have two offers on the property. This other buyer has been very tough to deal with. They are only giving the sellers four hours to decide. Do you want to call your clients to see if they'd like to improve their offer?"

Really? Are you kidding me right now? The first buyers are livid when they hear the news, suspecting foul play. They are very sour about the way this has been handled and not sure who to blame. In the back of their minds, they are questioning whether their own agent may have dropped the ball in this process. They really wanted this home. They tell their agent they need some time to discuss how they'd like to proceed.

They really didn't want to compete against another buyer for the property. That was the whole point of submitting a great offer as quickly as they did. They ask their agent how much time they have, assuming the same twenty-four hours would have been required for the second offer they were asked to provide. Not so much, unfortunately. They are even more upset when their agent tells them the second buyer has only given the sellers four hours to decide. Why did they give so much time when they submitted their offer? Well, the reason was, that was what the listing agent asked for and the buyer's agent agreed to it because they were trying to be respectful of the sellers being "out of town." They believed what the listing agent was saying and got burned by it.

So, what can they do about it now? Not much at this point. The only option the first buyers have if they really want the house is to improve their offer before the listing agent presents the other offer to the sellers, which will be at 6:45 p.m. It is now 5:30 p.m.

After forty-five minutes of heated discussions, the first buyers decide that although they really want to buy the property, they are going to leave their original offer as is. They believe it was a very fair offer and because it is an older home, they don't feel comfortable removing the home inspection condition. At 6:15 p.m. the first buyer's agent calls the listing agent to let them know their clients have decided to stand with their first offer. They would like it to be presented to the sellers as is.

At 6:30 p.m. the listing agent meets with the sellers to present both offers. Obviously, they are drawn towards the higher priced offer, but the listing agent very quickly points out that it does have a condition for the home inspection. He points out that, given their home is older, it is very likely the home inspector is going to find problems and the buyers are likely going to come back and try to renegotiate the price or ask them to make repairs. Either way, it is going to be a hassle for them.

The listing agent advises his clients that the wiser choice would be for them to go with the sure thing, which is the lower priced offer with no conditions. Besides, if they go with his offer, he can offer a further discount on the commission because he is double ending the deal and won't be splitting the commission with another brokerage.

The listing agent tells their clients "If we keep it between us," he can offer them a reduction on the commission which would save them close to $10,000. From this perspective, it would mean they are really getting $835,000 for their home and it is a sure thing with no unknowns. Interestingly, this discount is not mentioned to the first buyer's agent. "There's no point in taking a chance with that home inspection condition in the first offer," the listing agent tells the sellers. He reminds them, "it wouldn't take very long to make up the difference in repairs when the home inspector finds problems with the house."

They Needed Time to Think!

The sellers are very torn because they could really use the extra cash to put towards their new place and, besides, as far as they know there is nothing seriously wrong with their house. Nevertheless, the idea of a firm deal does sound very appealing. They can sleep at night knowing their home is sold, and they can start planning to move into that new dream home knowing everything is wrapped up with the sale of their current home. They'd like some time to think about it before they decide.

"Time to think about it? Sorry," the listing agent says. "We don't have any time for that. If you are planning to accept the first offer, we need to sign it before 7:00 p.m." Isn't it funny how they waited so long to present that first offer?

"That gives us less than fifteen minutes to sign and accept the first offer and send it back to the buyers, if that is what you want to do. If you do need more time, then we would have to send back a counteroffer and I wouldn't recommend we do that because if we do there is always a chance they could say, 'no.' And if they do, the second offer could also be expired by then. Just remember, there is no guarantee they would come back with a new offer. You might find yourself with no offers on the table. My suggestion would be to just keep it simple and accept the second offer."

Disappointed about accepting the lower, but firm offer, the sellers grudgingly accepted the listing agent's offer and respectfully declined the first buyer's offer. The listing agent then calls the first buyer's agent to break the bad news. "Sorry but unfortunately, my clients have decided to go with another offer. Please tell your clients we appreciated their offer and wish them all the best."

"How much did it sell for?" The buyer's agent asks. "You know I can't disclose that information," the listing agent says sheepishly. You'll just have to wait for the information to get posted in the system.

Three days later the listing is still showing as active in the MLS system and the first buyers are anxious to find out what the house sold for. The listing agent has been "too busy" to update the listing information. The buyers have asked their agent to keep them informed but so far haven't heard a word. Again, they question whether their agent has dropped the ball.

Growing impatient and frustrated, they decide to take matters into their own hands. They call the listing agent directly and ask what the home sold for. "Oh, didn't your agent let you know? I guess they must be too busy. It sold firm, for $825,000.

I put the information in our system three days ago. I am very sorry you didn't get the house, but I know of another very similar home that might be going on the market very soon. If you think you might be interested, I'd be happy to take you in to see it."

As you can imagine the first buyers are steamed that the house sold for $20,000 less than what they offered. They feel they were robbed! "How could this possibly have happened?" They feel their agent clearly wasn't competent! They are going to get to the bottom of this one. Who can they complain to? "I'm calling the brokerage. Someone is going to pay!"

And on the story goes. I think you get the point. Like most industries, I suppose, there are a few bad actors in real estate who grab the spotlight. Those are the ones who don't mind bending the rules or even outright ignoring them all together. They rely on the inaction of the people who suffer because of their unethical behavior and disregard for the rules. They think they can get away with it because no one is going to notice or, even if they do, they don't know what to do about it or they won't take the time to complain to the regulatory authorities. No one wants the hassle of going through that whole process. Who would bother? So, nothing happens, and the bad behavior continues.

People who've gone through an experience like this believe all real estate salespeople are like this. They think we are all the same. And they are not afraid to tell their friends and anyone else who will listen. That is why the real estate industry has such a bad reputation. The good news, thankfully, is that most real estate representatives are ethical, honest and conduct themselves like professionals.

If there is one thing I hope to accomplish from writing this book, it is to help improve the level of professionalism in the real estate industry by pointing out the obvious. It is up to each of us in the real estate industry to raise the bar in terms of our professionalism and the level of service we provide to our clients. We must treat each other and our clients with respect. Be honest and ethical in everything we do. Put our clients' best interests ahead of our own. Give 100% of our effort to everything we do. Commit to becoming the best version of ourselves we can possibly be. Never compromise our morals for even one deal. Commit to living our life and running our business by the Golden Rule and always treat others the way we would like to be treated. If we do that, everything is going to be just fine!

Chapter 19

Give Back to Your Community

It's not how much we get in life, it is how much we give,
that is the best measure of our success!
—Wayne Throop

If you ask me, one of the most important things every real estate representative should develop is a giving spirit. In fact, I would go so far as to say that giving back to your community is a big part of how I define "success." If you look around our industry, you'll see that most "successful" real estate representatives are extremely generous in their support of various charities.

The Royal LePage Shelter Foundation is the cause I support. I love the fact that 100% of all donations go straight to the organization's mission, which is to provide safe shelter for abused women and children. So far, this charity has raised more than $46,000,000 to support 200 women's shelters. But you can choose whatever cause is important to you. Maybe it is your church or cancer research. Maybe it is a children's hospital or your local food bank. Maybe it is a homeless shelter or the Snowsuit Fund, a charity in Ottawa, Ontario, that gives thousands of snowsuits every year to children in need. The actual cause you support is not as important as the fact that you are giving back.

We are very fortunate in our business. If you are a "successful" real estate representative who is close to the top of our industry, chances are you are earning a very good income. If you look at how we compare to other careers, the typical after-tax household income in Canada and the United States is well below $100,000. Meanwhile, top real estate representatives are likely to be earning substantially more than that on their own. The top 3% in our industry are likely earning three-to-four times more.

With all the craziness going on in the world today—from global pandemics, climate change, food shortages, inflation, high interest rates, and wars—there are more people who are suffering and in need of help than ever before. We must realize how fortunate and blessed we truly are here in North America. Not only are we living in one of the richest societies in the world, but if you are a successful real estate representative you are at the top of the top. You are very likely among the top income earners in the entire world. In short, you are able to do something to help those who are less fortunate and struggling. I believe that being a "success" is about more than just acquiring more stuff for yourself. It is about more than owning a nicer, bigger home. More than owning newer, fancier cars. More than just owning the best and most expensive clothes. Going on longer, more expensive, exotic vacations. It is about more than just padding your bank account and building your own personal net worth. Don't get me wrong, I am not against doing those things, I think they are all very important to many people. But I believe it is equally important to do what you can to help others who may be less fortunate than you are. Find a cause you believe in and do what you can to support it. To me, true success means you can live comfortably and provide for your family but also give back a portion of your earnings to support a cause that assists those who need it most.

When you do decide on which cause to support, I suggest you do it quietly. There is no need to shout, "Look at me! I support this local charity. How great is that?" That is more about your ego and less about genuinely supporting a cause you believe in. Do it because you want to help, not because you need the recognition. How much you give is up to you, but I would say at least 10% of your profits would be a reasonable target. If you can do more, even better, but do as much as you possibly can. There are a lot of people out there who are suffering.

The Value of Giving Back

Throughout my real estate career, I've been fortunate enough to be part of a company that values giving back to the community and helping those in need. It has been a core value of our firm since the day I joined. Now that I think about it, more than twenty years later, maybe that is the main reason why I've stayed with this company as long as I have. I certainly share that value with the company's leaders. I am not sure whether I adopted that value as a result of working for the company for so many years or perhaps I was always like that. Regardless, it is a core value that has also driven me to write this book.

Over the years, I can tell you I have attended many fundraising events held by both our local brokerage and our national firm. I have witnessed first-hand the generosity of our top agents who have donated hundreds of thousands of dollars to support the Royal LePage Shelter Foundation as well as various other charities. I've always tried to do the best I can to help as much as possible, but I wanted to do more.

In writing this book, it is my sincere desire to encourage you to give as much as you possibly can to support the people in our communities who need our help. I hope I can convince you that giving back is as important to your success as anything else you are going to do in this business. If you ask me, developing a giving spirit—and being committed to doing what you can to help others who may not be as fortunate as you are—is what true success looks like.

Chapter 20

A Few Interesting Real Estate Stories

Every day is a new adventure in the real estate business.
You just never know what might come up!
—Wayne Throop

If you like variety, real estate might just be the perfect place for you. No two days are ever the same. Just when you think you've seen or heard it all, something new happens and surprises you. No doubt most real estate representatives who have been around this business for any length of time will have countless interesting and funny stories to tell. I thought I'd share a few memorable moments from my own career in real estate.

If You're Not Busy, Just Plan Something!

One of my favorite stories happened early on in my career as a Broker/Manager. At the time, I had an agent in my office who had been in the business for a few years and was just starting to enjoy some success in her real estate business. She was a young mom who had two young kids and had planned a family vacation at Disney World in Orlando for the first time. It was to be a celebration of her recent success and a treat for her family to make up for some of the craziness she had put them through recently because of her real estate business.

As fate would have it, the night before her trip she received multiple offers on one of her listings. It was unfortunate timing but that seems to be the way it goes in real estate. As I like to say to agents, if you are ever not busy, just plan something. The second unfortunate part of this story is that she was not able to wrap things up the night before so the final decision to accept one of the offers was not made by her client until early in the morning when she was scheduled to board her flight. She was at the airport when I got the frantic call. I heard her panic-stricken voice on the other end as she said to me, "Wayne, I need your help! I don't know what to do. I had multiple offers on my listing last night. My client only made a final decision a few minutes ago. I'm late for my flight. They are calling our names on the overhead speakers telling us it is our last call to board our flight. My daughter just vomited chocolate milk all over the floor, so I handed my cell phone to my husband and asked him to text the agent whose offer we had accepted and let them know before we boarded the plane. Unfortunately, he was in a rush, and he mistakenly sent the text to the wrong agent!"

I said "Pardon"? "Did I just hear that correctly? You are late for your flight? Your daughter just threw up all over the floor at the airport? And your husband used your phone and texted the wrong agent to confirm that your client has accepted their offer?" And you're asking me what to do? Really?

I was a little stunned, to say the least. After a brief pause to think about this situation for a second, I quickly told her not to worry. "Just get on your flight and go enjoy your vacation. Send me the agents' names and a copy of the accepted offer and I will take care of this for you. Oh, and make sure you tell me the correct name of the agent who's offer you accepted."

After getting off the phone, I thought to myself "What have I done? How am I possibly going to fix this mess?" I am not exactly sure how I did it but, somehow, I called the buyer's agent and explained what had happened. After an initial outburst of rage and upset, I was able to calm everyone down and reach the desired outcome. To my surprise, it wasn't as hard as I expected. Everyone seemed to be fairly understanding and accepting of the situation once I explained it to them. A couple of them even had a chuckle about it. As they say, "all's well that ends well!"

Be Careful Who is Covering for You!

One of the biggest sources of conflict between real estate salespeople relates to disputes over commissions. Typically, when a real estate representative goes on a vacation, they will arrange for a colleague to cover for them while they are away. Normally, there would be some form of agreement between the two agents outlining how the agent who is covering will be paid. Often, they are given a referral fee on any deals they put together while the other agent is away.

One time, while I was the broker/manager of a real estate office, an agent from my office went away on a vacation and made arrangements with another agent from our office to cover for them while they were on vacation. They were going to be gone for three weeks. About halfway through that time, the agent who was covering had a unique and exciting opportunity come up unexpectedly and they, too, decided to go on vacation. They arranged for a third agent to cover for them, but they neglected to inform the agent that they were already covering for another agent. So, Agent #3 didn't know they were covering for both Agent #2 and Agent #1. As you can imagine, this whole scenario became very messy when an offer was received on one of Agent #1's listings. Unfortunately, Agent #1 and Agent #3 had no formal agreement in terms of how Agent #3 would be compensated. Agent #3 was anticipating receiving 50% of the listing commission but Agent #1 had only offered to pay 25% to Agent #2. This resulted in a lot of confusion and major conflict between the three agents involved.

The moral of this story is: make sure you have a written agreement overseen by a broker/manager outlining the details of who is covering for you and how they are being compensated.

The Key is Not in the Lock Box!

There was a time when I was working with a red-hot buyer, anxiously searching for a new home. The perfect house came up and we quickly booked a showing to go see it. We tried to be the first buyers to see that new listing, but it turned out someone else beat us to it. We got the second appointment right after the first one.

When we arrived, the door was locked and guess what? The key was missing from the lock box! I called the listing brokerage to let them know and they said they would reach out to the first buyer's agent. In the meantime, we had to reschedule our viewing appointment. After several attempts and a couple of hours the listing brokerage finally spoke to that buyer's agent. They were very sorry, but they had "forgotten" to return the key to the lock box. Unfortunately, they were completely booked for most of that day and wouldn't be able to return the key until late in the afternoon.

My buyers were annoyed and very anxious to go see that home. They wanted to see it as soon as possible. Then guess what happened? Three hours later the first buyer submitted a full-price offer with no conditions, with a short irrevocable period. The seller accepted their offer, and my buyers were left feeling extremely upset and crying foul!

Guest Book in the Primary Bedroom

There was a time when I was working with elderly, very spunky, single woman who was a real firecracker. She was very young at heart and acted much younger than her years. We found a home for sale that caught her interest, and we booked an appointment to see it. She had asked me to do some research about the listing and I was able to find out that a single woman lived in the house on her own. When we first arrived, everything appeared to be quite normal. It was a nice place. Clean and well cared for. My client had a witty sense of humor and was often cracking jokes. As she walked into the primary bedroom, I heard a chuckle. Then she said, "Wow! Someone has been busy! There is a guest book on the bedside table in the primary bedroom!" Who needs a guest book in their bedroom?

The Big Bad Wolf is in the Basement

Normally when an agent books an appointment to show a house to a client, they will receive an appointment confirmation from the listing brokerage through their phone. This appointment confirmation message will provide the date and time of the appointment, the lock box code, if there is one, and any special instructions or warnings the agent needs to be aware of.

I had booked a showing for a townhome one day in a popular local suburb and when I got the confirmation message with all the normal information, there was a note at the end that said: "There is a wolf in the basement. Do not attempt to enter the room with the door closed." I said "Pardon? There is a wolf in the basement?" Who has a wolf in their basement?

When I arrived at the property, I was explaining a few details about the home to my clients and then at the end I slipped in, "oh, and apparently there is a wolf in the basement."

They said "Pardon? There is a *what* in the basement?" "A wolf!" I said.

We proceeded cautiously through the home and there was not a peep from the basement. We went tippy-toeing down the stairs to the basement and whispered in soft voices to avoid disturbing the wolf. As we reached the bottom of the stairs, I saw "the room" with the closed door. I was tempted to just go and open it to prove there was no wolf, but I didn't, just in case. We quietly checked out the rest of the basement being careful not to wake that big bad wolf. We were cautious, but I don't think any of us truly believed there was actually a wolf in the room with the closed door. I suspect there must have been something in that room they didn't want anyone to see but I doubt very much it was a wolf. Honestly, you'd think they could have come up with something better than that!

There is an Offer on the Table!

It is not uncommon for an agent to tell a colleague they have an "offer on the table" but it is not very common to hear a client say that. One time, when I was selling residential properties, I had a client looking for a high-end home in a posh estate neighborhood with large homes on two-acre wooded lots. Privacy was very important to this lady and as far as I knew she had the funds she needed to buy one. This client was a little odd (perhaps some might even say eccentric). After working with her for a few weeks I began to think of her as the "crazy lady."

She would often cancel our appointments on very short notice and always had some kind of dramatic excuse for canceling. She would say things like: "I can't make it because my husband just had a massive heart attack," or, "my sister in-law was killed in a car accident last night," or, "my mother was just informed she has terminal cancer... My brother's house just burnt down, and he needs a place to stay... I fell down the stairs and broke my leg... " It was always something drastic. I am not suggesting she was lying but if all those things really did happen, this woman must have had the worst luck of anyone I had ever met.

One day she asked me to show her a beautiful property that had been listed for sale for a few weeks. As luck would have it, on our way to go see the property, I received a call from the listing brokerage to let me know they had received an offer on the property, but they had not accepted anything yet and that it would be okay for us to go ahead with our viewing appointment. As we walked into the kitchen, I heard my client say "Oh, I see they have an offer on the table." I happened to be looking the other way and I said to her, "yes, that is correct, the listing brokerage called me on my way here to let me know. I was just about to tell you that. How did you know?"

As I turned around, I saw her sitting at the kitchen table with an offer in her hand looking at the details on the front page. I was horrified! It turned out the homeowner had received the offer alright, and they had inadvertently left it out on the kitchen table in plain sight. My client said to me, "well at least if I do make an offer, I know how much I am going to have to pay now!" Fortunately, she decided she was not interested.

Don't Mention Offer Details in a Voicemail

Do you remember those old answering machines? The ones where you could hear the person leaving a message? Once I was showing a home to a potential buyer who was very interested. While we were in the house, the phone rang, and the listing agent began to leave a detailed voicemail message telling the homeowner they had received a great offer and proceeded to provide most of the major details. My client couldn't believe their luck! As it turned out, my client ultimately decided not to proceed with an offer, but we had a good laugh about it.

Are They Hiding in the Closet?

Selling a home can be an emotional and stressful experience. Many homeowners have a lot of pride in their homes, and they are curious to hear what agents and potential buyers say about their homes. They want "feedback."

On one occasion, the homeowner whose listing I had went to extremes to hear what people had to say. I had hosted an agent-only Open House where agents from different real estate brokerages were invited to come by to see my newest listing and give me their feedback on the property. About twelve agents came to the Open House that day and many made comments or asked questions while they were in the home.

Later that day my client called and started asking me about very specific comments made by some of the agents who had visited his home that morning. At the time, I remember I was surprised by how specific he was. How did he know exactly what the agents had said? When I asked, he brushed off my question and changed the subject. I continued to press him on it. He finally admitted that he had hidden in one of the closets during the Open House so he could hear what the agents had to say about his home. Now that is taking it to the next level. Can you imagine what would have happened if one of the agents had opened that closet door?

Chapter 21

Conclusion

If you have a positive attitude, a strong work ethic, integrity, patience and a lot of persistence, you might just have what it takes to make it to the top in the real estate industry!
—Wayne Throop

I've covered a lot of ground in this book, providing you with my interpretation of what the real estate industry is truly like behind the scenes and what I believe you need to be, do, and have to succeed at a high level in this industry.

I set out to accomplish two things. First, I wanted to help people who may be considering a career in real estate sales to make an informed decision. Secondly, I shared some of my own personal experiences and presented what I believe it will take to be a successful real estate representative and potentially make it to the top of this industry.

There are definitely a lot of people who want to give a career in real estate a try. They naively believe they have what it takes to do well in the business without really knowing what it is going to take to get them there. The truth is real estate is not a get-rich-quick scheme. It is far tougher than it looks and very few who start out in this business eventually make it to the top. Most don't even survive the first two years in the business. They get frustrated. They run out of money and then must go get a "real job" to pay the bills. Many of them probably never should have started in the first place. It is often a costly and frustrating adventure that ends in disappointment. It is my sincere hope that by writing this book, I have provided you with enough insight to make an informed decision about whether a career in real estate sales is right for you.

I believe that if you are considering a career in real estate sales, it's important to think of it as a marathon, not a sprint. It's a long-term game. Achieving a high level of success is going to require time. It is going to require a lot of patience and persistence. It is also going to require a lot of hard work and dedication and a firm commitment to personal growth and continuous improvement. It is not going to be easy. But for those select few who have what it takes, who put in the hard work and are focused on continuously improving themselves and their real estate business, this can be one of the most rewarding careers you can possibly imagine.

Every day will be a new adventure, a new opportunity to go out and serve others at the highest possible level. You will be acting as a trusted advisor, guiding people through the biggest financial transaction most will ever make in their entire lives. It's an opportunity to give back to your community, helping those who are less fortunate than you are. That is what I believe true success as a real estate agent looks like and it can become a powerful vehicle for a productive and fulfilling life. We each have the opportunity to stand as sentinels for professionalism and integrity in the business world and I think that's what our clients are asking us to do. This field has so much to offer us, from a financial and a personal perspective, and I invite you to join me in responding in kind by building real estate businesses that support the families and communities we have the privilege to serve. It's a demanding challenge. But what more could anyone ask for?

Bibliography

1. Cabral, Dr. Stephen. *The Rain Barrel Effect: How a 6,000-Year-Old Answer Holds the Secret to Finally Getting Well, Losing Weight & Feeling Alive Again!* Scotts Valley: CreateSpace, 2018.

2. Covey, Stephen R. *7 Habits of Highly Effective People: Powerful Lessons in Personal Change.* New York: Simon & Schuster.1989.

3. Elrod, Hal. *The Miracle Morning: The Not-So-Obvious Secret Guaranteed to Transform Your Life (Before 8 AM).* Self-published. 2012.

4. Goleman, Daniel. *Emotional Intelligence: Why It Can Matter More Than IQ.* New York: Bantam. 2005.

5. Hall, Doug. *The Maverick Mindset: Finding the Courage to Journey from Fear to Freedom.* New York: Simon & Schuster.1997.

6. Miller, Donald. *Building A Story Brand: Clarify Your Message So Customers Will Listen.* Nashville: Harper Collins Leadership. 2017.

7. Voss, Chris. *Never Split the Difference: Negotiating as If Your Life Depended on It.* New York: Harper Business Books. 2016

Acknowledgements

Writing and publishing a book is a massive project and a lengthy journey that could never be done alone. It takes courage, commitment, and lot of persistence to see it through to the finished product. But more than anything it takes people who will support and encourage you along the way. People who will guide you through the process and pick you up and dust you off and get you back on track when life's adversities come your way. You also need mentors, teachers, and colleagues to inspire you with stories and ideas to include in your book. Fortunately for me, I've benefited from all of the above.

This book would not have been possible without the wisdom, knowledge, support, and encouragement of many different people. There were however a select few who were instrumental in helping me cross the finish line.

First, I would like to thank Carole Blackburn who is a Life and Wellness Coach. It was her encouraging words that actually got me started on the journey to write this, my first, book. It was a long rocky road to travel, but I am grateful that you gave me that nudge I needed to get started. Thank you so much Carole!

Next, I would like to thank my Editor and Book Coach: Susan Crossman. It was her encouraging words that kept me going during my darkest days when it seemed my book writing project had lost all momentum. Her insights and guidance were invaluable throughout the research, planning, and writing process. Thank you so much, Susan. Without you this book would not have been possible.

I am extremely grateful to the Founder and Broker/Owner of the real estate brokerage I work for, Mr. Kent Browne. Kent has been one of my biggest fans and was actually the first person who read my initial draft. His feedback and suggestions were extremely helpful for me in improving the content of this book. Thank you, Kent—I appreciate your confidence in me and all you did to help me move this project forward.

I'd like to thank the many mentors I relied on to provide me with the ideas and inspiration to write this book. That list includes Brian Buffini, Richard Robbins, Zig Ziglar, Jim Rohn, Les Brown, Dr. Joe Dispenza, Bob Proctor, Michael Baylin, Rocco Manfredi, and many others.

I'd like to thank my family for their understanding when I was spending so many hours working on this project and perhaps not spending as much time with them as they might have liked. My Mom, Lorraine, who recently passed away, my partner, Michelle, my stepdaughter, Carley, and my step boys, Jacob and Joshua. Thank you for your understanding, support, and encouragement.

I would like to give special thanks to my many colleagues at Royal LePage Team Realty who provided valuable input, stories and suggestions that dramatically improved the final version of this book.

Thank you so much to everyone who some way helped me on this journey. I am eternally grateful for all your contributions to the successful completion of this book.

About Wayne Throop

Wayne Throop is a Real Estate Broker, Training Manager & Business Coach who has been a part of Royal LePage since 2004. Starting as a Sales Representative in 2004 in Ottawa, Ontario, he quickly became one of the company's top real estate representatives.

Between 2004-2010 he was in the Top 5% of Agents in his company across Canada five times earning several sales awards including the Directors Platinum award twice in 2006 & 2007 and then the Diamond Sales award three consecutive years from 2008-2010.

Starting in 2011, Wayne's real estate career shifted from sales to management when he became a Broker/Manager specializing in coaching, training and mentoring new agents. His real estate sales experience proved to be a big asset in ensuring new agents are successful in starting their real estate careers.

In addition to working closely with the newer agents, Wayne does one-on-one coaching with experienced agents and hosts several mastermind groups. He is an award winning Buffini Certified Mentor who was the 2023 Buffini Mentor of the Year.

He was voted as the Top Career Coach in Ottawa by Faces Magazine in 2022. He is also a certified trainer with Richard Robbins International. With his extensive experience in the real estate industry, Wayne is uniquely qualified to help Agents succeed in this challenging career path.

For more information visit:

www.waynethroop.com
https://www.facebook.com/RLPWayneThroop/
https://www.linkedin.com/in/wayne-throop-76344239/

Have you found value in what you've read?
Reviews are the life of a good book!
(we will place a link here)

Milton Keynes UK
Ingram Content Group UK Ltd.
UKHW031000231024
450026UK00011B/694